The Burden of Southern History

C. VANN WOODWARD

The Burden
of
Southern History

THIRD EDITION

LOUISIANA STATE UNIVERSITY PRESS
Baton Rouge and London

Copyright © 1960, 1968, 1991, 1993 by C. Vann Woodward
All rights reserved
Manufactured in the United States of America
First Printing
02 01 00 99 98 97 96 95 94 93   5 4 3 2 1

Library of Congress Cataloging-in-Publication Data

Woodward, C. Vann (Comer Vann), date.
    The burden of southern history / C. Vann Woodward. — 3rd ed.
     p. cm.
    Includes index.
    ISBN 0-8071-1894-X (alk. paper). — ISBN 0-8071-1891-5 (pbk. :
alk. paper)
    1. Southern States—Civilization. I. Title.
F209.5.W66 1993
975—dc20   93-29604
                                       CIP

TO

Robert Penn Warren

in memoriam

Contents

Preface to the Third Edition

THE TWO REVISIONS OF THE ORIGINAL EDITION OF 1960, THE first in 1968 and this, the second, have had much the same purpose: to test the validity of the two thematic essays, "The Search for Southern Identity" and "The Irony of Southern History." How have these essays and the others illustrating and supporting them held up against the winds of change and met the tests of time? What modifications, if any, have become necessary, and must concessions be made to critics?

To answer these questions I have in both revised editions called to witness developments that are more national and recent than Southern and historical in character and may therefore seem less related to the subjects suggested by the book's title. The fact is, however, that from the start the book was addressed to Southern history as it relates to and differs from national experience and myth, and to the past as it relates to the present.

In the 1968 revision two essays were added. The first, "What Happened to the Civil Rights Movement," addresses changes and racial relations, violent and nonviolent, as they have affected Southern identity and the irony of the regional experience. The other, "A Second Look at the Theme of Irony," uses the war in Vietnam as a test of the themes of both the South's distinctiveness and the ironies of its history, in both of which certain modifications are considered.

The present edition adds three more essays. For inspiring the chief of them I am indebted to John B. Boles. As editor of *The Journal of Southern History* he invited my reflections on "The Irony of Southern History" for the fortieth anniversary of its original publication in *The Journal* in 1953. I responded with the essay "Look Away, Look Away," giving special attention to how the theme of irony accommodates the changes that four decades have brought to Southern identity and distinctiveness, and the changes in racial relations.

In the earlier editions of the book I have made it a point to acknowledge the debt I think Southern historians owe to the eruption of creative energy in the region that was known in arts and letters as the Southern Renaissance. Novelists in particular seem responsible for having awakened a new and keener and more critical interest in regional history and a consciousness of the past in the present. Here I have singled out for tributes two writers, William Faulkner and Robert Penn Warren. I have had a more personal relationship with Warren than with Faulkner. It was to Warren that the book was dedicated in 1960, and it was to his express admonition to "accept the past and its burden" that my book owes its title.

C. V. W.

New Haven
August, 1993

Preface to the First Edition

THE EXAMPLES SET BY OTHERS WHO HAVE ATTEMPTED TO say why the heritage, or the collective character, or the general outlook of a particular geographical grouping of people is distinctive should constitute a warning to any who are disposed to try again. Few such efforts have stood up very well under the test of time. After a bit of aging, the parochial point of view, the temporal bias, or the didactic purpose begins to show through the pages more and more. Authority and conviction seep out of the writing, and it is soon forgotten. While this is not true of some efforts of the sort, it is true of a distressing proportion of them.

Perhaps the very nature of such enterprises makes for ephemerality. They are without doubt surrounded by formidable hazards. The quality of distinctiveness is notoriously elusive and often changes markedly over the years, sometimes under one's very eyes. Perhaps the most familiar illustration of the ephemerality of the popular national image is that of England since the sixteenth century. As the image changed from Elizabethan to Puritan, to Restoration, to Georgian, to Victorian, to Edwardian, John Bull contrived to run through as many stereotyped personalities as an operatic tenor has roles and costumes. The possibilities for embarrassment to theorists of national character are obviously numerous. Those who had proved to their own satisfaction that insular isolation, Anglo-Saxon blood, or foggy weather determined the English character were left to contrive even more ingenious theories to explain why the geography, the blood, or the climate did not change with the personality, or why the same circumstances produced such a bewildering variety of results.

Efforts to substantiate the familiar claim of a distinctive Southern heritage and explain what produced it have traditionally relied rather strongly on circumstance or situation, policy or purpose of the Southern people. In such accounts natural forces or man's will figure largely. Much has been made of climate, for example, and its supposed effect upon speech, manners, architecture, habits of work, and style of living in the South. Climate was a special favorite of nineteenth-century European theorists, who were naturally interested in explaining or perhaps justifying the conduct and character of imperialist enterprises of their period. Since these adventures often took place in the tropics or in climates quite different from those of England and Western Europe, the emphasis on climate was understandable. But the same blinding tropical sun that so readily explained a peculiar pattern of imperialist institutions in the nineteenth century shines upon a quite different pattern of institutions in the twentieth century. So it is in the South, where new and radically different institutions, architecture, crops, and styles of living flourish in the same old climate, environed by the same old geography.

Other theorists made much of race, the racial composition of the people, or racial attitudes and policies of the dominant race toward the subordinate race. Some writers found an entirely adequate key to Southern identity and character in the white man's purpose of maintaining racial integrity or white supremacy. But of recent decades racial composition of the Southern population has altered appreciably because of migrations and other reasons, and racial purposes and policy have altered or swayed under new influences.

The better studies of group or national character in late years have tended to go beyond circumstance and purpose, beyond natural environment and public policy, and to stress *experience* as the influence of first importance. Their focus has been upon the impact of experience and how it has been translated into personality and group character. Much experience of importance is private and individual in nature and would in the main seem best left to the psychologist for study. The historian is more properly concerned with the public and external forces that go to make up the collective experience and give shape to the group character of a people.

The experience of the South is, of course, complex and varied. This book is concerned only with such experience as contributed to the molding of a distinctive heritage and only with certain selective aspects of that experience. The essays that make up this collection were written at different times for different purposes during the past eight years, all but two of them in the last four years. It is hoped, nevertheless, that all of them have something to con-tribute to an understanding of the collective experience and the distinctive character of the South.

The first and last of the essays, "The Search for South-ern Identity" and "The Irony of Southern History," at-tack the question of what is peculiarly Southern more directly than do the others. "The Historical Dimension" turns to modern Southern letters for clues and definitions of the Southern heritage and its distinctiveness. In this and in all the essays the main comparison is with the North, or the non-Southern parts of America. The South is ob-viously American as well as Southern, and the first test of distinctiveness naturally lies in the establishment of a departure from the American norm.

The remaining essays deal with historical events or ex-periences that the South shared with the rest of America. But in each case the impact of the experience upon the South was markedly different from the impact registered upon other parts of the country. The Harpers Ferry Raid of 1859 was, to be sure, a national and not a regional event, and the prime movers, John Brown and his supporters, were about as Northern as they could well be. But the South's experience of that event was wholly different and distinct from that of the North. Similarly, the Civil War debate over equality for the Negro as "the third war aim," and the revolutionary aims framed for Reconstruction were of Northern origin, but the revolutionary impact of these movements and aims was very largely experienced in the South and not in the North. Likewise, the Populist movement was an event of national importance, but as a Southern experience it was largely felt as another alienation from the prevailing spirit in America. In these, as in other events, a common history has not necessarily meant a common experience, nor has it produced a uniformity of heritage and a conformity in character.

C. V. W.

Baltimore
May, 1960

Acknowledgments

FOR PERMISSION TO REPRINT THE ESSAYS THAT HAVE already appeared I am grateful to the original publishers:

"The Search for Southern Identity" was first published in *The Virginia Quarterly Review,* XXXIV (1958), 321–38.

"The Historical Dimension" was first published in *The Virginia Quarterly Review,* XXXII (1956), 258–67.

"John Brown's Private War" was prepared for a lecture at Bennington College and published along with other lectures in the same series, in *America in Crisis,* edited by Daniel Aaron (New York: Alfred A. Knopf, 1952).

"Equality: the Deferred Commitment" was delivered at the 125th Anniversary of the founding of Gettysburg College and first published in *The American Scholar,* XXVII (1958), 459–72.

"The Political Legacy of the First Reconstruction" was first published in *The Journal of Negro Education,* XXVI (1957), 231–40.

"The Populist Heritage and the Intellectual" was first published in *The American Scholar,* XXVIII (1959), 55–72.

"What Happened to the Civil Rights Movement" was

first published in *Harper's Magazine,* CCXXXIV (January, 1967), 29–37.

"The Irony of Southern History" was a presidential address before the Southern Historical Association, first published in *The Journal of Southern History,* XIX (1953), 3–19.

"Look Away, Look Away" was first published in *The Journal of Southern History,* LIX (August, 1993).

"The Burden for William Faulkner" was first published as a review essay in *The New Republic* of August 23, 1993.

"The Burden for Robert Penn Warren" was first published in *Proceedings of the American Philosophical Society,* CXXXVI (1992), 151–55.

The Burden of Southern History

1

The Search for Southern Identity

THE TIME IS COMING, IF INDEED IT HAS NOT ALREADY arrived, when the Southerner will begin to ask himself whether there is really any longer very much point in calling himself a Southerner. Or if he does, he might well wonder occasionally whether it is worth while insisting on the point. So long as he remains at home where everybody knows him the matter hardly becomes an issue. But when he ventures among strangers, particularly up North, how often does he yield to the impulse to suppress the identifying idiom, to avoid the awkward subject, and to blend inconspicuously into the national pattern—to act the role of the standard American? Has the Southern heritage become an old hunting jacket that one slips on comfortably while at home but discards when he ventures abroad in favor of some more conventional or modish garb? Or is it perhaps an attic full of ancestral wardrobes useful only in connection with costume balls and play acting—staged primarily in Washington, D.C.?

Asking himself some similar questions about the New

England heritage, Professor George W. Pierson of Yale has come forth with some disturbing concessions about the integrity of his own region. Instead of an old hunting jacket, he suggests that we call New England "an old kitchen floor, now spatter-painted with many colors." He points out that roughly six out of every ten Connecticut "Yankees" are either foreign-born or born of foreign or mixed parentage, while only three have native forebears going as far back as two generations, and they are not necessarily New England forebears at that. "Like it or not," writes Pierson, "and no matter how you measure it—geographically, economically, racially or religiously, there is no New England Region today." It has become instead, he says, "an optical illusion and a land of violent contrast and change." And yet in spite of the wholesale and damaging concessions of his essay, which he calls "A Study in Denudation," he concludes that, "as a region of the heart and mind, New England is still very much alive."

One wonders if the Southerner, for his part, can make as many damaging admissions of social change and cultural erosion as our New England friend has made and come out with as firm a conclusion about the vitality of his own regional heritage. More doubt than assurance probably comes to mind at first. The South is still in the midst of an economic and social revolution that has by no means run its course, and it will not be possible to measure its results for a long time to come. This revolution has already leveled many of the old monuments of regional distinctiveness and may end eventually by erasing the very consciousness of a distinctive tradition along with the will to sustain it. The sustaining will and consciousness are also under the additional strain of a moral indictment against a discredited part of the tradition, an indictment more uncompromising than any since abolitionist times.

The Southerner may not have been very happy about many of those old monuments of regional distinctiveness that are now disappearing. He may, in fact, have deplored the existence of some—the one-horse farmer, one-crop agriculture, one-party politics, the sharecropper, the poll tax, the white primary, the Jim Crow car, the lynching bee. It would take a blind sentimentalist to mourn their passing. But until the day before yesterday there they stood, indisputable proof that the South was different. Now that they are vanished or on their way toward vanishing, we are suddenly aware of the vacant place they have left in the landscape and of our habit of depending upon them in final resort as landmarks of regional identification. To establish identity by reference to our faults was always simplest, for whatever their reservations about our virtues, our critics were never reluctant to concede us our vices and shortcomings.

It is not that the present South has any conspicuous lack of faults, but that its faults are growing less conspicuous and therefore less useful for purposes of regional identification. They are increasingly the faults of other parts of the country, standard American faults, shall we say. Many of them have only recently been acquired—could, in fact, only recently be afforded. For the great changes that are altering the cultural landscape of the South almost beyond recognition are not simply negative changes, the disappearance of the familiar. There are also positive changes, the appearance of the strikingly new.

The symbol of innovation is inescapable. The roar and groan and dust of it greet one on the outskirts of every Southern city. That symbol is the bulldozer, and for lack of a better name this might be called the Bulldozer Revolution. The great machine with the lowered blade symbolizes the revolution in several respects: in its favorite area of operation, the area where city meets country; in its relentless speed; in its supreme disregard for obstacles, its heedless methods; in what it demolishes and in what it builds. It is the advance agent of the metropolis. It encroaches upon rural life to expand urban life. It demolishes the old to make way for the new.

It is not the amount of change that is impressive about the Bulldozer Revolution so much as the speed and concentration with which it has come and with which it continues. In the decade of the forties, when urbanization was growing at a swift pace in the country as a whole, the cities of the South's fifty-three metropolitan areas grew more than three times as fast as comparable cities in the rest of the country, at a rate of 33.1 per cent as compared with 10.3 per cent elsewhere. For every three city dwellers in the South at the beginning of that decade there were four at the end, and for every five farm residents there were only four. An overwhelmingly rural South in 1930 had 5.5 millions employed in agriculture; by 1950, only 3.2 millions. A considerable proportion of these Southerners were moving directly from country to suburb, following the path of the bulldozer to "rurbanization" and skipping the phase of urbanization entirely. Rural Negroes, the most mobile of all Southerners, were more likely to move into the heart of the urban areas abandoned by the suburban dwellers. In the single decade of the forties the South lost a third of its rural-farm Negro population. If the same trend were continued through the present decade, it would reduce that part of the colored population to about one-fifth of the Negroes living in the region.

According to nearly all of the indices, so the economists find, economic growth of the South in recent years greatly exceeds the rate maintained in the North and East. The fact is the South is going through economic expansion and reorganization that the North and East completed a generation or more ago. But the process is taking place far more rapidly than it did in the North. Among all the many periods of change in the history of the South it is impossible to find one of such concentration and such substantive impact. The period of Reconstruction might appear a likely rival for this distinction, but that revolution was largely limited to changes in legal status and the ownership of property. The people remained pretty much where they were and continued to make their living in much the same way. All indications are that the bulldozer will leave a deeper mark upon the land than did the carpetbagger.

It is the conclusion of two Southern sociologists, John M. Maclachlan and Joe S. Floyd, Jr., that the present drive toward uniformity "with national demographic, economic, and cultural norms might well hasten the day when the South, once perhaps the most distinctively 'differ-

ent' American region, will have become in most such matters virtually indistinguishable from the other urban-
industrial areas of the nation."

The threat of becoming "indistinguishable," of being
submerged under a national steamroller, has haunted the
mind of the South for a long time. Some have seen it as
a menace to regional identity and the survival of a Southern heritage. Premonitions of the present revolution appeared during the industrial boom that followed the First
World War. Toward the end of the twenties two distinctive
attempts were made by Southerners to dig in and define
a perimeter of defense against further encroachment.

One of these entrenchments was that of the twelve
Southerners who wrote *I'll Take My Stand*. They sought
to define what they called "a Southern way of life against
what may be called the American or prevailing way," and
they agreed "that the best terms in which to represent
the distinction are contained in the phrase, Agrarian
versus Industrial." Agrarianism and its values were the
essence of the Southern tradition and the test of Southern
loyalty. Their credo held that "the whole way in which we
live, act, think, and feel," the humanist culture, "was
rooted in the agrarian way of life of the older South." They
called for "anti-industrial measures" which "might promise to stop the advances of industrialism, or even undo
some of them."

Even in 1930 the agrarians were prepared to admit "the
melancholy fact that the South itself has wavered a little
and shown signs of wanting to join up behind the common
or American industrial ideal." They admonished waverers

among the younger generation that the brave new South they contemplated would "be only an undistinguished replica of the usual industrial community."

Three decades later the slight "wavering" in the Southern ranks that disturbed the agrarians in 1930 would seem to have become a pell-mell rout. Defections came by the battalion. Whole regiments and armies deserted "to join up behind the common or American industrial ideal." In its pursuit of the American Way and the American Standard of Living the South was apparently doing all in its power to become what the agrarians had deplored as "only an undistinguished replica of the usual industrial community." The voice of the South in the 1950's had become the voice of the chamber of commerce, and Southerners appeared to be about as much absorbed in the acquirement of creature comforts and adult playthings as any other Americans. The twelve Southerners who took their stand in 1930 on the proposition that the Southern way stands or falls with the agrarian way would seem to have been championing a second lost cause. If they were right, then our questions would have already been answered, for the Southerner as a distinctive species of American would have been doomed, his tradition bereft of root and soil. The agrarian way contains no promise of continuity and endurance for the Southern tradition.

Two years before the agrarian pronouncement appeared, another attempt was made to define the essence of the Southern tradition and prescribe the test of Southern loyalty. The author of this effort was the distinguished historian, Professor Ulrich B. Phillips. His definition had no reference to economic institutions but was confined to a preoccupation with race consciousness. The essential theme of continuity and unity in the Southern heritage, wrote Professor Phillips, was "a common resolve indomitably maintained" that the South "shall be and remain a white man's country." This indomitable conviction could be "expressed with the frenzy of a demagogue or maintained with a patrician's quietude," but it was and had been from the beginning "the cardinal test of a Southerner and the central theme of southern history."

Professor Phillips' criterion of Southernism has proved somewhat more durable and widespread in appeal than that of the agrarians. It is not tied so firmly to an ephemeral economic order as was theirs. Nor does it demand—of the dominant whites, at least—any Spartan rejection of the flesh pots of the American living standard. Its adherents are able to enjoy the blessings of economic change and remain traditionalists at the same time. There are still other advantages in the Phillipsian doctrine. The traditionalist who has watched the Bulldozer Revolution plow under cherished old values of individualism, localism, family, clan, and rural folk culture has felt helpless and frustrated against the mighty and imponderable agents of change. Industrialism, urbanism, unionism, and big government conferred or promised too many coveted benefits. They divided the people and won support in the South, so that it was impossible to rally unified opposition to them.

The race issue was different. Advocates and agents of change could be denounced as outsiders, intruders, med-

dlers. Historic memories of resistance and cherished constitutional principles could be invoked. Racial prejudices,
aggressions, and jealousies could be stirred to rally massive
popular support. And with this dearly bought unity, which
he could not rally on other issues, the frustrated traditionalist might at last take his stand for the defense of all the
defiled, traduced, and neglected values of the traditional
order. What then is the prospect of the Phillipsian "cardinal test" as a bulwark against change? Will it hold fast
where other defenses have failed?

Recent history furnishes some of the answers. Since the
last World War old racial attitudes that appeared more
venerable and immovable than any other have exhibited a
flexibility that no one would have predicted. One by one,
in astonishingly rapid succession, many landmarks of racial discrimination and segregation have disappeared, and
old barriers have been breached. Many remain, of course
—perhaps more than have been breached—and distinctively Southern racial attitudes will linger for a long time.
Increasingly the South is aware of its isolation in these
attitudes, however, and is in defense of the institutions
that embody them. They have fallen rapidly into discredit
and under condemnation from the rest of the country and
the rest of the world.

Once more the South finds itself with a morally discredited Peculiar Institution on its hands. The last time
this happened, about a century ago, the South's defensive
reaction was to identify its whole cause with the one institution that was most vulnerable and to make loyalty to
an ephemeral aspect which it had once led in condemning

the cardinal test of loyalty to the whole tradition. Southerners who rejected the test were therefore forced to reject
the whole heritage. In many cases, if they were vocal in
their rejection, they were compelled to leave the South
entirely and return only at their peril. Unity was thus temporarily achieved, but with the collapse of the Peculiar
Institution the whole tradition was jeopardized and discredited for having been so completely identified with the
part abandoned.

Historical experience with the first Peculiar Institution
ought strongly to discourage comparable experiments with
the second. If Southernism is allowed to become identified
with a last ditch defense of segregation, it will increasingly
lose its appeal among the younger generation. Many will
be tempted to reject their entire regional identification,
even the name "Southern," in order to dissociate themselves from the one discredited aspect. If agrarianism has
proved to be a second lost cause, segregation is a likely
prospect for a third.

With the crumbling of so many defenses in the present,
the South has tended to substitute myths about the past.
Every self-conscious group of any size fabricates myths
about its past: about its origins, its mission, its righteousness, its benevolence, its general superiority. But few
groups in the New World have had their myths subjected
to such destructive analysis as those of the South have
undergone in recent years. While some Southern historians
have contributed to the mythmaking, others have been
among the leading iconoclasts, and their attacks have
spared few of the South's cherished myths.

The Cavalier Legend as the myth of origin was one of the earlier victims. The Plantation Legend of ante bellum grace and elegance has not been left wholly intact. The pleasant image of a benevolent and paternalistic slavery system as a school for civilizing savages has suffered damage that is probably beyond repair. Even the consoling security of Reconstruction as the common historic grievance, the infallible mystique of unity, has been rendered somewhat less secure by detached investigation. And finally, rude hands have been laid upon the hallowed memory of the Redeemers who did in the Carpetbaggers, and doubt has been cast upon the antiquity of segregation folkways. These faded historical myths have become weak material for buttressing Southern defenses, for time has dealt as roughly with them as with agrarianism and racism.

Would a hard-won immunity from the myths and illusions of Southern sectionalism provide some immunity to the illusions and myths of American nationalism? Or would the hasty divestment merely make the myth-denuded Southerner hasten to wrap himself in the garments of nationalism? The danger in the wholesale rejection of the South by the modern Southerner bent on reaffirming his Americanism is the danger of affirming more than he bargains for.

While the myths of Southern distinctiveness have been waning, national myths have been waxing in power and appeal. National myths, American myths have proved far more sacrosanct and inviolate than Southern myths. Millions of European immigrants of diverse cultural backgrounds have sought and found identity in them. The powerful urge among minority groups to abandon or disguise their distinguishing cultural traits and conform as quickly as possible to some national norm is one of the most familiar features in the sociology of American nationalism. European ethnic and national groups with traditions far more ancient and distinctive than those of the South have eagerly divested themselves of their cultural heritage in order to conform.

The conformist is not required nor expected to abandon his distinctive religion. But whether he remains a Protestant, a Catholic, or a Jew, his religion typically becomes subordinate or secondary to a national faith. Foreign observers have remarked that the different religions in America resemble each other more than they do their European counterparts. "By every realistic criterion," writes Will Herberg in his study of American religious sociology, "the American Way of Life is the operative faith of the American people." And where the mandates of the American Way of Life conflict with others, they take undisputed sway over the masses of all religions. Herberg describes it as "a faith that has its symbols and its rituals, its holidays and its liturgy, its saints and its sancta," and it is common to all Americans. "Sociologically, anthropologically, if one pleases," he writes, the American Way of Life "is the characteristic American religion, undergirding American life and overarching American society despite all indubitable differences of region, section, culture, and class." Differences such as those of region and section, "indubitable" though he admits them to be, he characterizes as "peripheral and obsolescent."

If the American Way of Life has become a religion, any deviation from it has become a sort of heresy. Regionalism in the typical American view is rather like the Turnerian frontier, a section on the move—or at least one that should keep moving, following a course that converges at not too remote a point with the American Way. It is a season's halt of the American caravan, a temporary encampment of an advancing society, eternally on the move toward some undefined goal of progress. If the encampment of regionalism threatens to entrench or dig in for a permanent stand, it comes to be regarded as "peripheral and obsolescent," an institutionalized social lag.

The same urge to conformity that operates upon ethnic or national minorities to persuade them to reject identification with their native heritage or that of their forebears operates to a degree upon the Southerner as well. Since the cultural landscape of his native region is being altered almost beyond recognition by a cyclone of social change, the Southerner may come to feel as uprooted as the immigrant. Bereft of his myths, his peculiar institutions, even his familiar regional vices, he may well reject or forget his regional identification as completely as the immigrant.

Is there nothing about the South that is immune from the disintegrating effect of nationalism and the pressure for conformity? Is there not something that has not changed? There is only one thing that I can think of, and that is its history. By that I do not mean a Southern brand of Shintoism, the worship of ancestors. Nor do I mean written history and its interpretation, popular and mythical, or professional and scholarly, which have changed

often and will change again. I mean rather the collective
experience of the Southern people. It is in just this respect
that the South remains the most distinctive region of the
country. In their unique historic experience as Americans
the Southerners should not only be able to find the basis
for continuity of their heritage but also make contributions that balance and complement the experience of the
rest of the nation.

At this point the risks of our enterprise multiply. They
are the risks of spawning new myths in place of the old.
Awareness of them demands that we redouble precautions
and look more cautiously than ever at generalizations.

To start with a safe one, it can be assumed that one of
the most conspicuous traits of American life has been its
economic abundance. From early colonial days the fabulous riches of America have been compared with the scarcity and want of less favored lands. Immense differentials
in economic welfare and living standards between the
United States and other countries still prevail. In an illu-
minating book called *People of Plenty,* David Potter persuasively advances the thesis that the most distinguishing traits of national character have been fundamentally
shaped by the abundance of the American living standard.
He marshals evidence of the effect that plenty has had
upon such decisive phases of life as the nursing and train-
ing of babies, opportunities for education and jobs, ages of
marriage and childbearing. He shows how abundance has
determined characteristic national attitudes between parents and children, husband and wife, superior and subordinate, between one class and another, and how it has

molded our mass culture and our consumer oriented society. American national character would indeed appear
inconceivable without this unique experience of abundance.

The South at times has shared this national experience
and, in very recent years, has enjoyed more than a taste of
it. But the history of the South includes a long and quite
un-American experience with poverty. So recently as 1938,
in fact, the South was characterized by the President as
"The Nation's Economic Problem No. 1." And the problem was poverty, not plenty. It was a poverty emphasized
by wide regional discrepancies in living standard, per
capita wealth, per capita income, and the good things that
money buys, such as education, health, protection, and the
many luxuries that go to make up the celebrated American
Standard of Living. This striking differential was no temporary misfortune of the great depression but a continuous and conspicuous feature of Southern experience since
the early years of the Civil War. During the last half of
the nineteenth and the first half of the twentieth centuries,
when technology was multiplying American abundance
with unprecedented rapidity, the South lagged far behind.
In 1880 the per capita wealth of the South, based on esti-
mated true valuation of property, was $376 as compared
with $1,186 per capita in the states outside the South. In
the same year the per capita wealth of the South was 27
per cent of that of the Northeastern states. That was just
about the same ratio contemporaneously existing between
the per capita wealth of Russia and that of Germany.

Generations of scarcity and want constitute one of the
distinctive historical experiences of the Southern people,

an experience too deeply embedded in their memory to be wiped out by a business boom and too deep not to admit of some uneasiness at being characterized historically as a "People of Plenty." That they should have been for so long a time a "People of Poverty" in a land of plenty is one mark of enduring cultural distinctiveness. In a nation known around the world for the hedonistic ethic of the American Standard of Living, the Southern heritage of scarcity remains distinctive.

A closely related corollary of the uniquely American experience of abundance is the equally unique American experience of success. During the Second World War Professor Arthur M. Schlesinger made an interesting attempt to define the national character, which he brought to a close with the conclusion that the American character "is bottomed upon the profound conviction that nothing in the world is beyond its power to accomplish." In this he gave expression to one of the great American legends, the legend of success and invincibility. It is a legend with a foundation in fact, for much can be adduced from the American record to support it and explain why it has flourished. If the history of the United States is lacking in some of the elements of variety and contrast demanded of any good story, it is in part because of the very monotonous repetition of successes. Almost every major collective effort, even those thwarted temporarily, succeeded in the end. American history *is* a success story. Why should such a nation not have a "profound conviction that nothing in the world is beyond its power to accomplish"? Even the hazards of war—including the prospect of war against an unknown enemy with untried weapons—proves no exception to the rule. The advanced science and weaponry of the Russian challenger are too recent to have registered their impact on the legend. The American people have never known the chastening experience of being on the losing side of a war. They have, until very recently, solved every major problem they have confronted—or had it solved for them by a smiling fortune. Success and victory are still national habits of mind.

This is but one among several American legends in which the South can participate only vicariously or in part. Again the Southern heritage is distinctive. For Southern history, unlike American, includes large components of frustration, failure, and defeat. It includes not only an overwhelming military defeat but long decades of defeat in the provinces of economic, social, and political life. Such a heritage affords the Southern people no basis for the delusion that there is nothing whatever that is beyond their power to accomplish. They have had it forcibly and repeatedly borne in upon them that this is not the case. Since their experience in this respect is more common among the general run of mankind than that of their fellow Americans, it would seem to be a part of their heritage worth cherishing.

American opulence and American success have combined to foster and encourage another legend of early origin, the legend of American innocence. According to this legend Americans achieved a sort of regeneration of sinful man by coming out of the wicked Old World and removing to an untarnished new one. By doing so they

shook off the wretched evils of feudalism and broke free
from tyranny, monarchism, aristocracy, and privilege—
all those institutions which, in the hopeful philosophy of
the Enlightenment, accounted for all, or nearly all, the
evil in the world. The absence of these Old World ills in
America, as well as the freedom from much of the injustice and oppression associated with them, encouraged a
singular moral complacency in the American mind. The
self-image implanted in Americans was one of innocence
as compared with less fortunate people of the Old World.
They were a chosen people and their land a Utopia on
the make. Alexis de Tocqueville's patience was tried by
this complacency of the American. "If I applaud the freedom which its inhabitants enjoy, he answers, 'Freedom
is a fine thing, but few nations are worthy to enjoy it.' If
I remark on the purity of morals which distinguishes the
United States," complained Tocqueville, " 'I can imagine,'
says he, 'that a stranger, who has been struck by corruption
of all other nations, is astonished at the difference.' "

How much room was there in the tortured conscience
of the South for this national self-image of innocence and
moral complacency? Southerners have repeated the American rhetoric of self admiration and sung the perfection
of American institutions ever since the Declaration of Independence. But for half that time they lived intimately
with a great social evil and the other half with its aftermath. It was an evil that was even condemned and abandoned by the Old World, to which America's moral superiority was supposedly an article of faith. Much of the
South's intellectual energy went into a desperate effort to

convince the world that its peculiar evil was actually a "positive good," but it failed even to convince itself. It writhed in the torments of its own conscience until it plunged into catastrophe to escape. The South's preoccupation was with guilt, not with innocence, with the reality of evil, not with the dream of perfection. Its experience in this respect, as in several others, was on the whole a thoroughly un-American one.

An age-long experience with human bondage and its evils and later with emancipation and its shortcomings did not dispose the South very favorably toward such popular American ideas as the doctrine of human perfectibility, the belief that every evil has a cure, and the notion that every human problem has a solution. For these reasons the utopian schemes and the gospel of progress that flourished above the Mason and Dixon Line never found very wide acceptance below the Potomac during the nineteenth century. In that most optimistic of centuries in the most optimistic part of the world, the South remained basically pessimistic in its social outlook and its moral philosophy. The experience of evil and the experience of tragedy are parts of the Southern heritage that are as difficult to reconcile with the American legend of innocence and social felicity as the experience of poverty and defeat are to reconcile with the legends of abundance and success.

One of the simplest but most consequential generalizations ever made about national character was Tocqueville's that America was "born free." In many ways that is the basic distinction between the history of the United States and the history of other great nations. We skipped the feudal stage, just as Russia skipped the liberal stage. Louis Hartz has pointed up the complex consequences for the history of American political thought. To be a conservative and a traditionalist in America was a contradiction in terms, for the American Burke was forever conserving John Locke's liberalism, his only real native tradition. Even the South, in its great period of reaction against Jefferson, was never able fully to shake off the grip of Locke and its earlier self-image of liberalism. That is why its most original period of theoretical inspiration, the "Reactionary Enlightenment," left almost no influence upon American thought.

There is still a contribution to be derived from the South's un-American adventure in feudal fantasy. While the South was not born Lockean, it went through a Lockean phase in its youth. But as Hartz admits, it was "an alien child in a liberal family, tortured and confused, driven to a fantasy life." There *are* Americans, after all, who were not "born free." They are also Southerners. They have yet to achieve articulate expression of their uniquely un-American experience. This is not surprising, since white Southerners have only recently found expression of the tragic potentials of their past in literature. The Negro has yet to do that. His first step will be an acknowledgment that he is also a Southerner as well as an American.

One final example of a definition of national character to which the South proves an exception is an interesting one by Thornton Wilder. "Americans," says Mr. Wilder, "are abstract. They are disconnected. They have a relation, but it is to everywhere, to everybody, and to always." This quality of abstraction he finds expressed in numerous ways —in the physical mobility of Americans, in their indifference or, as he might suggest, their superiority to place, to locality, to environment. "For us," he writes, "it is not *where* genius lived that is important. If Mount Vernon and Monticello were not so beautiful in themselves and relatively accessible, would so many of us visit them?" he asks. It is not the concrete but the abstract that captures the imagination of the American and gives him identity, not the here-and-now but the future. " 'I am I,' he says, 'because my plans characterize me.' Abstract! Abstract!" Mr. Wilder's stress upon abstraction as an American characteristic recalls what Robert Penn Warren in a different connection once described as "the fear of abstraction" in the South, "the instinctive fear, on the part of black or white, that the massiveness of experience, the concreteness of life, will be violated; the fear of abstraction."

According to Mr. Wilder, "Americans can find in environment no confirmation of their identity, try as they may." And again, "Americans are disconnected. They are exposed to all place and all time. No place nor group nor movement can say to them: we are waiting for you; it is right for you to be here." The insignificance of place, locality, and community for Thornton Wilder contrasts strikingly with the experience of Eudora Welty of Mississippi. "Like a good many other [regional] writers," she says, "I am myself touched off by place. The place where I am and the place I know, and other places that familiarity with and love for my own make strange and lovely and enlightening to look into, are what set me to writing my stories." To her, "place opens a door in the mind," and she speaks of "the blessing of being located—contained."

To do Mr. Wilder justice, he is aware that the Southern states constitute an exception to his national character of abstraction, "enclaves or residual areas of European feeling," he calls them. "They were cut off, or resolutely cut themselves off, from the advancing tide of the country's modes of consciousness. Place, environment, relations, repetitions are the breath of their being."

The most reassuring prospect for the survival of the South's distinctive heritage is the magnificent body of literature produced by its writers in the last three decades —the very years when the outward traits of regional distinctiveness were crumbling. The Southern literary renaissance has placed its writers in the vanguard of national letters and assured that their works will be read as long as American literature is remembered. The distinguishing feature of the Southern school, according to Allen Tate, is "the peculiar historical consciousness of the Southern writer." He defines the literary renaissance as "a literature conscious of the past in the present." The themes that have inspired the major writers have not been the flattering myths nor the romantic dreams of the South's past. Disdaining the polemics of defense and justification, they have turned instead to the somber realities of hardship and defeat and evil and "the problems of the human heart in conflict with itself." In so doing they have brought to realization for the first time the powerful literary potentials of the South's tragic experience and heritage. Such comfort as they offer lies, in the words of William Faulkner, in reminding us of "the courage and honor and hope and pride and compassion and pity and sacrifice" with which man has endured.

After Faulkner, Wolfe, Warren, and Welty no literate Southerner could remain unaware of his heritage or doubt its enduring value. After this outpouring it would seem more difficult than ever to deny a Southern identity, to be "merely American." To deny it would be to deny our history. And it would also be to deny to America participation in a heritage and a dimension of historical experience that America very much needs, a heritage that is far more closely in line with the common lot of mankind than the national legends of opulence and success and innocence. The South once thought of itself as a "peculiar people," set apart by its eccentricities, but in many ways modern America better deserves that description.

The South was American a long time before it was Southern in any self-conscious or distinctive way. It remains more American by far than anything else, and has all along. After all, it fell the lot of one Southerner from Virginia to define America. The definition he wrote in 1776 voiced aspirations that were rooted in his native region before the nation was born. The modern Southerner should be secure enough in his national identity to escape the compulsion of less secure minorities to embrace uncritically all the myths of nationalism. He should be secure enough also not to deny a regional heritage because it is at variance with national myth. It is a heritage that should prove of enduring worth to him as well as to his country.

2

The Historical Dimension

IT WOULD SEEM TO BE HIGH TIME FOR SOME SOUTHERN
historian to abandon temporarily the standoffishness of
his guild and make his bow to Southern men of letters.
Not that it is necessary at this late date to acknowledge
that the literary men have earned the greater acclaim and
distinction. That goes without saying. What is really
needed is some acknowledgment of the genuine debt the
historians owe to the poets, playwrights, and novelists—
particularly the novelists—as well as an acknowledgement
of vital relations between the crafts.

The generation of Southerners who went to college in
the 1920's usually took a defensive attitude toward the
history of their region, or affected indifference. It was an
attitude compounded of several factors: the college boy's
revolt against the ideas and values of his parents, the striving to cover up a consciousness of provincialism, and an
eagerness to appear abreast of the times, if not a little in
advance. Even so staunch a traditionalist as Donald Davidson admitted the force of these impulses when he wrote

in 1926: "The gallantries of the Lost Cause, the legends of Southern history—these he may admire, but they came to him mouthed over and cheapened . . . the treacly lamentations of the old school."

Being "old school" in the 1920's was the worst possible offense against the canons of the collegian, and he strove with all his might to avoid the charge. He readily gathered from the literary monitors of fashion and taste whom he admired that there was nothing issuing from his native region in the way of arts and letters that was worth his notice. When *The Sound and the Fury* appeared in 1929, the young Southerner was assured by the *New Republic* that it "signified nothing." He also absorbed the impression from numerous quarters that the history of the South was generally discreditable, if not faintly ridiculous. All things considered, it was not the most auspicious background for one who aspired to become a Southern historian.

The Southerner who was graduated from college about 1930 was soon aware of new voices in the land and new forces astir. He doubtless derived some encouragement from the contemporary awakening of historical scholarship, particularly if he hoped to be a historian. But it was soon apparent that the stir among historians was only a minor aspect of a wider intellectual awakening in the South. The most brilliant manifestation was in the field of letters and literary criticism. To mention only a few books of one author, within the three years beginning in 1929 there appeared William Faulkner's *Sartoris, The Sound and the Fury, As I Lay Dying, Sanctuary,* and

Light in August—a one-man renaissance by 1932. Katherine Anne Porter's first book, *Flowering Judas,* appeared in 1930. Shortly before that, there arose the bright star of Thomas Wolfe with the appearance of *Look Homeward, Angel.* Of all American novels, that is the book of the young man, especially the young Southerner, and no one who read it in his youth will forget the strange excitement of the experience. The early thirties were stirring years to be discovering the South and its history and spending the years of one's youth.

The spice of controversy and polemic was added by the Nashville manifesto, *I'll Take My Stand,* in 1930. Counterblast provoked counterblast, and the controversy raged on in the pages of Davidson's *Attack on Leviathan* and in successive numbers of the *American Review* and later in the *Southern Review.* With the establishment of the latter in 1935 the center of the avant garde of American literary criticism shifted temporarily to the banks of the Mississippi at Baton Rouge. Gradually the pundits and critical moguls on the Hudson began to alter their tone about the "Sahara of the Bozart." An occasional note of praise, then of cautious respect, was succeeded by fulsome acclaim and eventually by a sort of awed puzzlement at this sudden flowering of the cultural desert. The young Southerner took a vicarious pride in all this achievement, a pride that did wonders for his provincial inferiority complex. He hailed the new names as they appeared—Robert Penn Warren, Eudora Welty, Tennessee Williams—and new ones kept arriving on the scene.

Allen Tate spoke of this outpouring as "quite temporary"

in 1935 and thought that year marked "the height of the Southern literary renaissance." But in 1935 some of the brighter luminaries had not yet appeared on the horizon. Again, in 1945, Tate wrote that "that Renascence is over." But in 1955 Andrew Nelson Lytle could declare: "The Renascence has been going on for thirty years with little sign of diminishment." The fact is that we have grown up with this movement, and it will remain for a later generation to fix its limits and assess its achievements.

Our concern here is with its significance for the historian rather than with its place in history. It was early apparent that the new Southern writers had something special to say to the historian, something that no other living American writers—and few dead ones—seemed to say. If he had read any American literature in college, it was not likely to have been of Southern origin. The literary awakening of the Middle West was still in the public eye in the twenties, and the collegian of that era plowed through his Theodore Dreiser, Edgar Lee Masters, Sherwood Anderson, and Sinclair Lewis. There was little in their pages to increase his respect or deepen his appreciation for the uses of history. The characters in the novels of Dreiser, Anderson, and Lewis appear on the scene from nowhere, trailing no clouds of history, dissociated from the past. They seem to have left it behind them in New England, or Norway, or Bavaria, and along with their past they checked their forebears, their historical roots and associations. One has the feeling that they considered that heritage a good riddance. They rarely discuss it, and one gathers there was no room for it in such baggage as they brought along to Gopher Prairie, Winesburg, or Chicago.

In the work of some later writers the historical perspective is even more flat. Hemingway's characters appear to live completely in the present. To emphasize their historical rootlessness they are invariably pictured as expatriates, as wanderers, as soldiers or adventurers. They are temporarily in Italy or Spain, in France or Africa, in Cuba or the Florida Keys. A Hemingway hero with a grandfather is inconceivable, and he is apparently quite as bereft of uncles, aunts, cousins, and in-laws, not to mention neighbors and poor relations. With Dos Passos the story is somewhat different. But for all his marvelous gift for evoking a given place or a period of the recent past (a gift historians can but envy), his characters are exclusively preoccupied with personal problems or with social problems of their own time. They are haunted by no ghosts of the past, and the past does not seem to be part of the present. If our collegian was coached through a reading of the literary flowering of New England that took place a century or more ago, he will have discovered little more of the historical dimension than he found in the more recent schools. The New Englanders, with the exception of Hawthorne, regularly pictured the individual starkly alone with his problems, his wilderness, or his God. Cooper and Henry James offer a certain amount of historical depth, but the characters of Melville appear to live entirely in the present or the future and to concern themselves seldom with the past.

To discover the new school of Southern fiction after

1930 was to enter suddenly upon a new world of the imagination, a world in which the historical imagination played a supreme part. In his essay on "The Profession of Letters in the South," Allen Tate has fixed upon "the peculiarly historical consciousness of the Southern writer" as the secret spring of creative energies that has fed the whole literary movement in the South during the last three decades. Tate has also suggested an historical explanation for the intellectual awakening of the South and the heightening of historical consciousness so characteristic of it. He suggests that after the First World War the South arrived at a crossroads of history where an old traditional order was being rapidly obliterated and a new modern order was being simultaneously brought to birth. Caught at these crossroads, the Southerner was made more keenly conscious at once of the present and of the past. His sensitivity to the current change heightened his awareness of past differences, and his intensified remembrance of things past added corresponding poignancy to his awareness of things present. As Tate put it, "that backward glance gave us the Southern renascence, a literature conscious of the past in the present."

A claim to what Tate called "the peculiarly historical consciousness of the Southern writer" was made by Ellen Glasgow in her posthumously published autobiography. "I had been born," she wrote, "with an intimate feeling for the spirit of the past, and the lingering poetry of time and place." In the last volume of his ten-volume work, Arnold Toynbee advances the theory that "the vividness of historical impressions is apt to be proportionate to their vio-

lence and painfulness" and speculates that "a child who
had lived through the American Civil War in the territory of the Southern Confederacy would be likely to
grow up more historical-minded than one who had lived
through the same experience at the North." In this connection a statement of Katherine Anne Porter has some
relevance. "I am a grandchild of a lost War," she writes
in *The Days Before,* "and I have blood-knowledge of
what life can be in a defeated country on the bare bones
of privation."

In emphasizing the place that historical consciousness
plays in contemporary Southern writing, I have no reference to the vogue of the conventional historical novel.
The South has produced its share of the historical romance, and during the early years of the present century
when the market reached one of its peaks, Southern popular writers produced considerably more than their share
of best-sellers. But production figures reveal no particular
regional concentration. The Northern and Western writers have proved themselves as handy at this craft as the
Southern. Their product has little to do with Tate's "literature conscious of the past in the present." And it might
be observed parenthetically that modern craftsmen of that
school sometimes reverse Tate's description and tend at
times to interject a dubious awareness of the present in the
past. At any rate, we are not concerned here with the
historical romance—whether its purpose is to score some
point about the present or to settle some score about the
past.

It is interesting but quite tangential to the argument that

the first books of two leading figures of the Southern
Renaissance were not in the field of fiction but of history.
These were Allen Tate's biography of Stonewall Jackson,
published in 1928, and Robert Penn Warren's biography
of John Brown, published in 1929. It is also a source of
great fascination to the historian—though still neither
essential nor quite relevant to the thesis—that some of
our most gifted novelists have chosen historical periods or
figures or movements as subjects. Ellen Glasgow set out
early in her career to write what she described as "a social
history of Virginia" from 1850 to 1912. It must be admitted, however, that none of her "Novels of the Com-
monwealth," as she called them, are among her best
works. Faulkner has been engaged for the better part of
three decades in rounding out his Yoknapatawpha world
of McCaslins, Sartorises, and Compsons; its MacCallums,
Bundrens, and Snopeses; its Joe Christmases, Lucas Beau-
champs, and Charles Bons. While this saga so far represents the supreme creation of the Southern Renaissance,
it is not history in any usual sense. And it is not unlikely
that the Faulkner critics have gone astray in thinking
of the Yoknapatawpha novels as Southern history in micro-
cosm, or as representing any very consistent ideas or theories about Southern history. In the universality of their
meaning they are more, and in their immediate application
less, than that.

The Southern novelist who comes nearest approaching an historical subject after the manner of an historian
is Warren. Yet Warren is careful and perfectly correct to
warn the reader of *Night Rider* that "although this book

was suggested by certain events which took place in Kentucky in the early years of the century, it is not, in any strict sense, a historical novel." What Warren has pronounced "the boneheadedness or gospel-bit hysteria" of those who insist upon making either history or a political tract out of *All the King's Men* drives the author to despair. He quotes Louis Armstrong as remarking, "There is some folks that if they don't know, you can't tell 'em." While Warren selects the same sort of subject matter as the historian—the Black Patch War in Kentucky during the first decade of the century, a financial tycoon of Tennessee in the twenties, or a demagogue of Louisiana in the thirties —he could rightly say of them all, as he said of the first, that they are not historical novels in any strict sense. At the same time it could be as accurately said that they quicken and vivify our consciousness of history in a way that conventional historical novels, as well as many bona fide histories, do not.

The relevance of the theme of "historical consciousness" in Southern letters would have been the same had the novelists never tackled a historical subject or treated any period prior to Appomattox. It is not the period nor the subject that is the point but, in Tate's words, the consciousness of the past in the present. Here, among many possible illustrations, one thinks of Katherine Anne Porter's Miranda in *Old Mortality,* seeking through the years of her youth to find and come to terms with her family's past and her own past and to relate them to the present. Or of Thomas Wolfe's Eugene Gant, "the haunter of himself, trying for a moment to recover what he had been part of . . . a stone, a leaf, an unfound door," and lyrically imploring, "Ghost, come back again." Or of Faulkner's Quentin Compson in *Absalom, Absalom!* groping through the convolutions of Colonel Sutpen's incredible legend for an answer to Shreve McCannon's questions in 1910. Or of Warren's Jack Burden in *All the King's Men* brooding endlessly over the faded letters and diaries of Cass Mastern for a lost meaning to the past and a key to the present in the 1930's.

This preoccupation, this almost obsessive concern of Southern writers with the past in the present has been expressed often explicitly as well as implicitly in their stories. Thus John Peale Bishop wrote in his essay, "The South and Tradition," that "without a past we are living not in the present, but in a vague and rather unsatisfactory future." Katherine Anne Porter remarks of Miranda's family that "their hearts and imaginations were captivated by their past," but while the author never treats that past as such, it is constantly obtruding itself into the present she does treat. On the other hand, Ellen Glasgow did repeatedly treat historical episodes and epochs, but her most successful use of the past was probably in such unhistorical novels as *Barren Ground* and *The Sheltered Life*. For all his reference to the Old South, Faulkner has never attempted a full-bodied treatment of the Civil War, as much as it impinges on his major themes. His themes have been preponderantly those of the post bellum South. Still, he has Gavin Stevens say in *Intruder in the Dust,* "The past is never dead. It's not even past." In the course of a bear hunt we are taken all the way back to tribal life among the aborigines of Mississippi through Sam Fathers, their descendant. For the Southern school the present is a fleeting segment of the cumulative past and might be described by the concluding words of *All the King's Men:* ". . . out of history, into history and the awful responsibility of Time."

Another deeply embedded trait of the Southern novelists that has strong appeal to the historian is their way of treating man not as an individual alone with his conscience or his God, as the New Englanders were inclined to do, or alone at sea with a whale or a marlin, or alone in a ring with a bull, but as an inextricable part of a living history and community, attached and determined in a thousand ways by other wills and destinies of people he has only heard about. Herbert Marshall McLuhan has remarked that "the sense of belonging to a great chain of persons and events, passive yet responsible, is everywhere in Faulkner." And he quotes T. S. Stribling on "the chain of wrongs and violences out of which his life had been molded." In *Band of Angels* Warren has its narrator say, "You live through time, that little piece of time that is yours, but that piece of time is not only your own life, it is the summing-up of all the other lives that are simultaneous with yours." This, in sum, is also the way the historian tries to see the individual and the forces that mold him.

Francis B. Simkins has urged that "the historian of the South should join the social novelist who accepts the values of the age and section about which he writes." The trouble lies in the ambiguities of the verb "to accept." And there is also the question of which values and what age. Faulkner

certainly never accepted the values of the Snopeses, nor
of the Compsons either. For it is just the tragedy of the
Compsons in *The Sound and the Fury* that in the person
of Jason Compson they *did* accept the values of the age
—the age of the Snopeses. The historian like the novelist
should not change his values with his ages, whether it is
the age of Colonel Sutpen or of Jason Compson. This was
precisely the mistake of the John B. Gordons and Basil
Dukes and their generation. They did.

The best of the Southern novelists have never set out to
defend the values or the prejudices or the errors of any
particular age or section. It is true that their books are often
filled with tales of horror and lust and betrayal and degradation. But they have not paused to reckon their popularity
in attacking the values of their own age or any other. They
have not set up as defenders of a cause, either one lost or
one still sought. They have proved themselves able to confront the chaos and irony of history with the admission
that they can fit them into no neat pattern and explain
them by no pat theory.

The historian is fortunate, I think, in sharing a period
with literary men of great talent who share so many of his
own values, so much of his own outlook and point of view,
and so much of his own subject matter. He can afford to
take pride in their achievements and comfort in their
example. This is no plea for the relaxation of the severe
limitations of the historian's discipline, nor for his bor-
rowing the novelist's license. But once the historian aban-
dons an old and false analogy with the natural sciences
and sees that his craft employs no special concepts nor

categories nor special terminology, he will admit that he attempts to "explain" history in the same way he explains events in ordinary life—his own as well as that of his fellow men—and with much the same language, moral and psychological. He should then acknowledge that Southern men of letters have advanced many of the aims he shares. They have helped us penetrate the romantic haze of an older generation as well as the cynical stereotypes of our own. They have endowed the denigrated and emotionally impoverished New South with a sense of tragedy and dignity that history had hitherto reserved for the Old Régime, and they have enriched our consciousness of the past in the present. They have helped to bring the Negro into intelligible focus without the glasses of sentimentality. And they have given history meaning and value and significance as events never do merely because they happen. These are things the historian also strives to do, and he should seek to do them with the same fortitude and honesty.

3

John Brown's Private War

THE FIGURE OF JOHN BROWN IS STILL WRAPPED IN OBSCUR-
ity and myth. In the fourteen biographies of Brown published since 1859, the legend makers have done their part,
but much of the difficulty is inherent in the nature of
Brown's life and character. His fifty-nine years were divided sharply into two periods. The obscurity of his first
fifty-five years was of the sort natural to a humble life
unassociated with events of importance. The obscurity of
his last four years, filled with conspiratorial activities, was
in large part the deliberate work of Brown, his fellow
conspirators, and their admirers.

Poverty and failure haunted the first fifty-five years of
John Brown's life. The father of twenty children, he was
compelled to see his family drag along in want and at
times in something approaching destitution. In thirty-five
years he was engaged in more than twenty different business ventures in six states. Most of them ended in failure,
some in bankruptcy, and at least two in crime. Brown was
involved for years as defendant in one litigation after an-

other brought against him for failure to meet his financial obligations. "Several of the cases in question leave no doubt of flagrant dishonesty on his part in both business and family relations," concludes Professor James C. Malin. The historian suggests that "this record of unreliability proven in court" might serve as "an index to the reliability of John Brown as a witness after he became a public character." The remarkable thing about this record is that it seems to have interfered in no way with the second of his careers. After 1855 John Brown abandoned his unprofitable business career when he was almost penniless and for the rest of his life was without remunerative employment. He depended for support upon donations from people whom he convinced of his integrity and reliability. Here and elsewhere there is strong evidence that Brown was somehow able to inspire confidence and intense personal loyalty.

The Kansas phase of Brown's guerrilla warfare has given rise to the "Legend of Fifty-six," a fabric of myth that has been subjected to a more rigorous examination than any other phase of Brown's life has ever received. Malin establishes beyond question that "John Brown did not appear to have had much influence either in making or marring Kansas history," that his exploits "brought tragedy to innocent settlers," but that "in no place did he appear as a major factor." He also establishes a close correlation between the struggle over freedom and slavery and local clashes over conflicting land titles on the Kansas frontier, and he points out that "the business of stealing horses under the cloak of fighting for freedom and running them off to the Nebraska-Iowa border for sale" is a neglected aspect of the struggle for "Bleeding Kansas." John Brown and his men engaged freely and profitably in this business and justified their plunder as the spoils of war. Two covenants that Brown drew up for his followers contained a clause specifically providing for the division of captured property among the members of his guerrilla band.

It would be a gross distortion, however, to dismiss John Brown as a frontier horse thief. He was much too passionately and fanatically in earnest about his war on slavery to permit of any such oversimplification. His utter fearlessness, courage, and devotion to the cause were greatly admired by respectable antislavery men who saw in the old Puritan an ideal revolutionary leader.

One exploit of Brown in Kansas, however, would seem to have put him forever beyond the pale of association with intelligent opponents of slavery. This was the famous Pottawatomic massacre of May 24, 1856. John Brown, leading four of his sons, a son-in-law, and two other men, descended by night upon an unsuspecting settlement of four proslavery families. Proceeding from one home to another the raiders took five men out, murdered them, and left their bodies horribly mutilated. None of the victims was a slaveholder, and two of them were born in Germany and had no contact with the South. By way of explanation Brown said the murders had been "decreed by Almighty God, ordained from Eternity." He later denied responsibility for the act, and some of the Eastern capitalists and intellectuals who supported him refused to believe him guilty. In view of the report of the murders that was laid

before the country on July 11, 1856, in the form of a committee report in the House of Representatives, it is somewhat difficult to excuse such ignorance among intelligent
men.

It was shortly after this report was published, however,
that, for his war on slavery, Brown enjoyed his most striking success in soliciting contributions and making friends
among men of wealth and intellectual distinction in Boston and other Eastern cities. In the first four months of
1858 he succeeded in raising $23,000 in cash, supplies, and
credit to support his guerrilla activities.

In the spring of 1858 plans for a raid on Virginia began
to take definite shape. To a convention of fellow conspirators in Chatham, Canada, in May, John Brown presented his remarkable "Provisional Constitution and Ordi-
nances for the People of the United States." It represented
the form of government he proposed to establish by force
of arms with a handful of conspirators and an armed insurrection of slaves. Complete with legislative, executive,
and judicial branches, Brown's revolutionary government
was in effect a military dictatorship, since all acts of his
congress had to be approved by the commander-in-chief
of the army in order to become valid. Needless to say, John
Brown was elected commander-in-chief.

By July, 1859, Commander-in-Chief Brown had established himself at a farm on the Maryland side of the Potomac River, four miles north of Harpers Ferry. There he
assembled twenty-one followers and accumulated ammuni-
tion and other supplies, including 200 revolvers, 200 rifles,
and 950 pikes specially manufactured for the slaves he

expected to rise up in insurrection. On Sunday night, October 16, after posting a guard of three men at the farm, he set forth with eighteen followers, five of them Negroes, and all of them young men, to start his war of liberation and found his abolitionist republic. Brown's first objective, to capture the United States arsenal at Harpers Ferry, was easily accomplished since it was without military guard. In the Federal armory and the rifle works, also captured, were sufficient arms to start the bloodiest slave insurrection in history.

The commander-in-chief appears to have launched his invasion without any definite plan of campaign and then proceeded to violate every military principle in the book. He cut himself off from his base of supplies, failed to keep open his only avenues of retreat, dispersed his small force, and bottled the bulk of them up in a trap where defeat was inevitable. "In fact, it was so absurd," remarked Abraham Lincoln, "that the slaves, with all their ignorance, saw plainly enough it could not succeed." Not one of them joined Brown voluntarily, and those he impressed quickly departed. The insurrectionists killed one United States Marine and four inhabitants of Harpers Ferry, including the mayor and a Negro freeman. Ten of their own number, including two of Brown's sons, were killed, five were taken prisoner by a small force of Marines commanded by Robert E. Lee, and seven escaped, though two of them were later arrested. John Brown's insurrection ended in a tragic and dismal failure.

When news of the invasion was first flashed across the country, the most common reaction was that this was obviously the act of a madman, that John Brown was insane. This explanation was particularly attractive to Republican politicians and editors, whose party suffered the keenest embarrassment from the incident. Fall elections were on, and the new Congress was about to convene. Democrats immediately charged that John Brown's raid was the inevitable consequence of the "irresistible-conflict" and "higher-law" abolitionism preached by Republican leaders William H. Seward and Salmon P. Chase. "Brown's invasion," wrote Senator Henry Wilson of Massachusetts, "has thrown us, who were in a splendid position, into a defensive position. . . . If we are defeated next year we shall owe it to that foolish and insane movement of Brown's." The emphasis on insanity was taken up widely by Wilson's contemporaries and later adopted by historians.

It seems best to deal with the insanity question promptly, for it is likely to confuse the issue and cause us to miss the meaning of Harpers Ferry. In dealing with the problem it is important not to blink, as many of his biographers have done, at the evidence of John Brown's close association with insanity in both his heredity and his environment. In the Brown Papers at the Library of Congress are nineteen affidavits signed by relatives and friends attesting the record of insanity in the Brown family. John Brown's maternal grandmother and his mother both died insane. His three aunts and two uncles, sisters and brothers of his mother, were intermittently insane, and so was his only sister, her daughter, and one of his brothers. Of six first cousins, all more or less mad, two were deranged from time to time, two had been repeatedly committed to the state insane asylum, and two were still confined at the time. Of John Brown's immediate family, his first wife and one of his sons died insane, and a second son was insane at intervals. On these matters the affidavits, signers of which include Brown's uncle, a half brother, a brother-in-law, and three first cousins, are in substantial agreement. On the sanity of John Brown himself, however, opinion varied. Several believed that he was a "monomaniac," one that he was insane on subjects of religion and slavery, and an uncle thought his nephew had been "subject to periods of insanity" for twenty years.

The insurrectionist himself, of course, stoutly maintained that he was perfectly sane, and he was certainly able to convince many intelligent people, both friend and foe, that he was sane. He firmly refused to plead insanity at his trial. Governor Henry A. Wise of Virginia went so far as to write out orders to the superintendent of the state insane asylum to examine Brown, but endorsed the orders, "countermanded upon reflection." On the other hand, John Brown pronounced Governor Wise mad. "Hard to tell who's mad," jested Wendell Phillips to a laughing congregation in Henry Ward Beecher's church. "The world says one man's mad. John Brown said the same of the Governor. . . . I appeal from Philip drunk to Philip sober." He meant future generations when, he said, "the light of civilization has had more time to penetrate." Then it would be plain that not Brown but his enemies were mad.

We, the Philips sober of the future, with some misgivings about how far "the light of civilization" has penetrated, do think we know a little more about insanity than did our great-grandfathers. We at least know that it is a loose expression for a variety of mental disorders and that it is a relative term. What seems sane to some people at some times seems insane to other people at other times. In our own time we have witnessed what we consider psychopathic personalities rise to power over millions of people and plunge the world into war. Yet to the millions who followed them these leaders appeared sublime in their wisdom.

"John Brown may be a lunatic," observed the Boston *Post,* but if so, "then one-fourth of the people of Massachusetts are madmen," and perhaps three-fourths of the ministers of religion. Begging that Brown's life be spared, Amos A. Lawrence wrote Governor Wise: "Brown is a Puritan whose mind has become disordered by hardship and illness. He has the qualities wh. endear him to our people." The association of ideas was doubtless unintentional, but to the Virginian it must have seemed that Lawrence was saying that in New England a disordered mind was an endearing quality. The Reverend J. M. Manning of Old South Church, Boston, pronounced Harpers Ferry "an unlawful, a foolhardy, a suicidal act" and declared, "I stand before it wondering and admiring." Horace Greeley called it "the work of a madman" for which he had not "one reproachful word," and for the "grandeur and nobility" of which he was "reverently grateful." And the New York *Independent* declared that while "Harpers Ferry was insane, the controlling motive of this demonstration was sublime." It was both foolhardy and godly, insane and sublime, treasonous and admirable.

The prestige and character of the men who lent John Brown active, if sometimes secret, support likewise suggest caution in dismissing Harpers Ferry as merely the work of a madman. Among Brown's fellow conspirators the most notable were the so-called Secret Six. Far from being horse thieves and petty traders, the Secret Six came from the cream of Northern society. Capitalist, philanthropist, philosopher, surgeon, professor, minister—they were men of reputability and learning, four of them with Harvard degrees.

With a Harvard Divinity School degree, a knowledge of twenty languages, and a library of sixteen thousand volumes, Theodore Parker was perhaps the most prodigiously learned American of his time. In constant correspondence with the leading Republican politicians, he has been called "the Conscience of a Party." What Gerrit Smith, the very wealthy philanthropist and one-time congressman of Peterboro, New York, lacked in mental endowments he made up in good works—earnest efforts to improve the habits of his fellow men. These included not only crusades against alcohol and tobacco in all forms, but also coffee, tea, meat, and spices—"almost everything which gave pleasure," according to his biographer. Generous with donations to dietary reform, dress reform, woman's rights, educational and "non-resistance" movements, Smith took no interest whatever in factory and labor reform, but he was passionately absorbed in the antislavery movement and a liberal contributor to John Brown. Dr. Samuel G. Howe of Boston, husband of the famous Julia Ward Howe, was justly renowned for his humanitarian work for the blind and mentally defective. In his youth he had gone on a Byronic crusade in Greece against the Turk. These experiences contributed greatly to his moral prestige, if little to his political sophistication. The most generous man of wealth among the conspirators was George L. Stearns of Boston, a prosperous manufacturer of lead pipe. In the opinion of this revolutionary capitalist, John Brown was "the representative man of this century, as Washington was of the last." Finally there were two younger men, fledgling conspirators. The son of a prosperous Boston merchant who was bursar of Harvard, Thomas Wentworth Higginson became pastor of a church in Worcester after taking his divinity degree at Harvard. Young Franklin B. Sanborn was an apostle of Parker and a protégé of Emerson, who persuaded Sanborn to take charge of a school in Concord.

The most tangible service the Secret Six rendered the conspiracy lay in secretly diverting to John Brown, for use at Harpers Ferry, money and arms that had been contributed to the Massachusetts-Kansas Aid Committee for use in "Bleeding Kansas." This dubious transaction was accomplished by Stearns, chairman of the committee, exercising as a private individual an option he held of foreclosing upon the property of the committee, then promptly transferring the arms to Brown and notifying only the conspirators. By this means the Kansas Committee was converted into a respectable front for subversive purposes, and thousands of innocent contributors to what appeared to be a patriotic organization discovered later that they had furnished rifles for a treasonous attack on a Federal arsenal. Even Sanborn admitted in 1885 that "it is still a little difficult to explain this transaction concerning the arms without leaving the suspicion that there was somewhere a breach of trust." It still is.

The Secret Six appear to have been fascinated by the drama of conspiratorial activity. There were assumed names, coded messages, furtive committee meetings, dissembling of motives, and secret caches of arms. And over all the romance and glamor of a noble cause—the liberation of man. Although they knew perfectly well the general purpose of Brown, the Secret Six were careful to request him not to tell them the precise time and place of the invasion. The wily old revolutionist could have told them much that they did not know about the psychology of fellow travelers. Brown had earlier laid down this strategy for conspirators who were hard pressed: "Go into the houses of your most prominent and influential white friends with your wives; and that will effectually fasten upon them the suspicion of being connected with you, and will compel them to make a common cause with you, whether they would otherwise live up to their professions or not." The same strategy is suggested by Brown's leaving behind, in the Maryland farmhouse where they would inevitably be captured, all his private papers, hundreds of letters of himself and followers, implicating nobody knew how many respectable fellow travelers.

When news of the captured documents arrived, there

occurred a very unheroic panic among the Secret Six, who saw stark ruin and an indictment for treason facing them. Stearns, Sanborn, and Howe fled to Canada. Parker was already abroad. Gerrit Smith's secretary did not stop until he reached England. Smith himself issued pitiable and panicky denials of his guilt, then found refuge in insanity and was confined to an asylum. Howe published a denial unworthy of respect. Higginson alone stood his ground. Stearns and Howe denied any knowledge of the attack before a congressional committee, and both of them told Sanborn they "found the question of the Senate Committee so unskillfully framed that they could, without literal falsehood, answer as they did."

The assistance that the Secret Six conspirators were able to give John Brown and his Legend was as nothing compared with that rendered by other Northern intellectuals. Among them was the cultural and moral aristocracy of America in the period that has been called a "Renaissance." Some of these men, Ralph Waldo Emerson and Henry Thoreau among them, had met and admired Brown and even made small contributions to his cause. But they were safely beyond reproach of the law and were never taken into his confidence in the way that the Secret Six were. Their service was rendered after the event in justifying and glorifying Brown and his invasion.

In this work the intellectuals were ably assisted by a genius, a genius at self-justification—John Brown himself. From his prison cell he poured out a stream of letters, serene and restrained, filled with Biblical language and fired with overpowering conviction that his will and God's were one and the same. These letters and his famous speech at the trial constructed for the hero a new set of motives and plans and a new role. For Brown had changed roles. In October he invaded Virginia as a conqueror armed for conquest, carrying with him guns and pikes for the army he expected to rally to his standard and a new constitution to replace the one he overthrew. In that role he was a miserable failure. Then in November he declared at his trial: "I never did intend murder, or treason, or the destruction of property, or to excite or incite slaves to rebellion, or to make an insurrection." He only intended to liberate slaves without bloodshed, as he falsely declared he had done in Missouri the year before. How these statements can be reconciled with the hundreds of pikes, revolvers, and rifles, the capture of an armory, the taking of hostages, the killing of unarmed civilians, the destruction of government property, and the arming of slaves is difficult to see. Nor is it possible to believe that Brown thought he could seize a Federal arsenal, shoot down United States Marines, and overthrow a government without committing treason. "It was all so thin," as Robert Penn Warren has observed of the trial speech, "that it should not have deceived a child, but it deceived a generation." At Lincoln's funeral Emerson compared it with the Gettysburg Address.

Emerson seemed hesitant in his first private reactions to Harpers Ferry. Thoreau, on the other hand, never hesitated a moment. On the day after Brown's capture he compared the hero's inevitable execution with the crucifixion of Christ. Harpers Ferry was "the best news that America ever had"; Brown, "the bravest and humanest man in all the country," "a Transcendentalist above all," and he declared: "I rejoice that I live in this age, that I was his contemporary." Emerson quickly fell into line with Thoreau, and in his November 8 lecture on "Courage" described Brown as "the saint, whose fate yet hangs in suspense, but whose martyrdom, if it shall be perfected, will make the gallows as glorious as the cross." Within a few weeks Emerson gave three important lectures, in all of which he glorified John Brown.

With the Sage of Concord and his major prophet in accord on the martyr, the majority of the transcendental hierarchy sooner or later joined in—William E. Channing, Bronson and Louisa May Alcott, Longfellow, Bryant, and Lowell, and of course Wendell Phillips and Theodore Parker. Parker pronounced Brown "not only a martyr" . . . but also a SAINT." Thoreau and Henry Ward Beecher frankly admitted they hoped Brown would hang. To spare a life would be to spoil a martyr. They were interested in him not as a man but as a symbol, a moral ideal, and a saint for a crusade. In the rituals of canonization the gallows replaced the cross as a symbol. Louisa May Alcott called the gallows "a stepping-stone to heaven"; Parker, "the road to heaven"; Theodore Tilton, "a throne greater than a king's"; and Phillips concluded that "henceforth it is sacred forever."

Among Western antislavery men there were fewer intellectuals of fame or notoriety, but abolitionist preachers, teachers, and orators joined in apotheosizing Brown. Citizens of Oberlin erected a monument to three Negroes who gave their lives in Brown's raid. And Theodore D.

Weld, once the genius of Western abolitionism, though in retirement, permitted burial of two of the Harpers Ferry raiders at his school in New Jersey. Not all of the Northern intellectuals became members of the Brown cult. Nathaniel Hawthorne and Walt Whitman were two notable dissenters. Devotees of the cult showed little tolerance for dissent. Emerson declared that "all people, in proportion to their sensibility and self-respect, sympathize with him [Brown]," and Thoreau carried intolerance to the point of moral snobbery. "When a noble deed is done, who is likely to appreciate it? They who are noble themselves," answered Thoreau. "I was not surprised that certain of my neighbors spoke of John Brown as an ordinary felon, for who are they? They have either much flesh, or much office, or much coarseness of some kind. They are not ethereal natures in any sense. The dark qualities predominate in them. . . . For the children of the light to contend with them is as if there should be a contest between eagles and owls."

The task to which the intellectuals of the cult dedicated themselves was the idealizing of John Brown as a symbol of the moral order and the social purpose of the Northern cause. Wendell Phillips expressed this best when he declared in the Boston Music Hall: "'Law' and 'order' are only means for the halting ignorance of the last generation. John Brown is the impersonation of God's order and God's law, moulding a better future, and setting for it an example." In substituting the new revolutionary law and order for traditional law and order, the intellectuals encountered some tough problems in morals and values. It was essential for them to justify a code of political methods and morals that was at odds with the Anglo-American tradition.

John Brown's own solution to this problem was quite simple. It is set forth in the preamble of his Provisional Constitution of the United States, which declares that in reality slavery is an "unjustifiable War of one portion of its citizens upon another." War, in which all is fair, amounted to a suspension of ethical restraints. This type of reasoning is identical with that of the revolutionaries who hold that class struggle is in reality a class war. The assumption naturally facilitates the justification of deeds otherwise indefensible. These might include the dissembling of motives, systematic deception, theft, murder, or the liquidation of an enemy class.

It is clear that certain enthusiasts found in Brown's reasoning a satisfactory solution to their moral problem, but it was equally clear that the mass of people were not yet ready to accept this solution and that some other rationalization was required. The doctrine of the "Higher Law" and the doctrine of "Civil Disobedience" had already done much to prepare the way for acceptance of the revolutionary ethics. They had justified conduct in defiance of the Constitution and the government by appeal to higher moral ends. Transcendental doctrine was now used to extend the defiance of tradition even further. Thoreau's reply to attacks upon John Brown's methods was: "The method is nothing; the spirit is all." This was the Transcendentalist way of saying that means are justified by the ends. According to this doctrine, if the end is sufficiently noble—as noble as the emancipation of the slave—any means used to attain the end is justified.

The crisis of Harpers Ferry was a crisis of means, not of ends. John Brown did not raise the question of whether slavery should be abolished or tolerated. That question had been raised in scores of ways and debated for a generation. Millions held strong convictions on the subject. Upon abolition, as an *end*, there was no difference between John Brown and the American and Foreign Anti-Slavery Society. But as to the *means* of attaining abolition, there was as much difference between them, so far as the record goes, as there is between the modern British Labour Party and the government of Soviet Russia on the means of abolishing capitalism. The Anti-Slavery Society was solemnly committed to the position of nonviolent means. In the very petition that Lewis Tappan, secretary of the society, addressed to Governor Wise in behalf of Brown he repeated the rubric about "the use of all carnal weapons for deliverance from bondage." But in their rapture over Brown as martyr and saint the abolitionists lost sight of their differences with him over the point of means and ended by totally compromising their creed of nonviolence.

But what of those who clung to the democratic principle that differences should be settled by ballots and that the will of the majority should prevail? Phillips pointed out: "In God's world there are no majorities, no minorities; one, on God's side, is a majority." And Thoreau asked, "When were the good and the brave ever in a majority?" So much for majority rule. What of the issue of treason?

The Reverend Fales H. Newhall of Roxbury declared that the word "treason" had been "made holy in the American language"; and the Reverend Edwin M. Wheelock of Boston blessed "the sacred, and the radiant 'treason' of John Brown."

No aversion to bloodshed seemed to impede the spread of the Brown cult. William Lloyd Garrison thought that "every slaveholder has forfeited his right to live" if he impeded emancipation. The Reverend Theodore Parker predicted a slave insurrection in which "The Fire of Vengeance" would run "from man to man, from town to town" through the South. "What shall put it out?" he asked. "The White Man's blood." The Reverend Mr. Wheelock thought Brown's "mission was to inaugurate slave insurrection as the divine weapon of the antislavery cause." He asked: "Do we shrink from the bloodshed that would follow?" and answered, "No such wrong [as slavery] was ever cleansed by rose-water." Rather than see slavery continued the Reverend George B. Cheever of New York declared: "It were infinitely better that three hundred thousand slaveholders were abolished, struck out of existence." In these pronouncements the doctrine that the end justifies the means had arrived pretty close to justifying the liquidation of an enemy class.

The reactions of the extremists have been stressed in part because it was the extremist view that eventually prevailed in the apotheosis of John Brown and, in part, because by this stage of the crisis each section tended to judge the other by the excesses of a few. "Republicans were all John Browns to the Southerners," as Professor Dwight

L. Dumond has observed, "and slaveholders were all Simon Legrees to the Northerners." As a matter of fact Northern conservatives and unionists staged huge anti-Brown demonstrations that equaled or outdid those staged by the Brown partisans. Nathan Appleton wrote a Virginian: "I have never in my long life seen a fuller or more enthusiastic demonstration" than the anti-Brown meeting in Faneuil Hall in Boston. The Republican press described a similar meeting in New York as "the largest and most enthusiastic" ever held in that city. Northern politicians of high rank, including Lincoln, Douglas, Seward, Edward Everett, and Henry Wilson, spoke out against John Brown and his methods. The Republican party registered its official position by a plank in the 1860 platform denouncing the Harpers Ferry raid. Lincoln approved of Brown's execution, "even though he agreed with us in thinking slavery wrong." Agreement on ends did not mean agreement on means "That cannot excuse violence, bloodshed, and treason," said Lincoln.

Republican papers of the Western states as well as of the East took pains to dissociate themselves from Harpers Ferry, and several denounced the raid roundly. At first conservative Southern papers, for example the *Arkansas State Gazette,* rejoiced that "the leading papers, and men, among the Black Republicans, are open . . . in their condemnation of the course of Brown." As the canonization of Brown advanced, however, the Republican papers gradually began to draw a distinction between their condemnation of Brown's raid and their high regard for the man himself—his courage, his integrity, and his noble motives.

They also tended to find, in the wrongs Brown and his men had suffered at the hands of slaveholders in Kansas, much justification for his attack upon Virginia. From that it was an easy step to pronounce the raid a just retribution for the South's violence in Kansas. There was enough ambiguity about Republican disavowal of Brown to leave doubts in many minds. If Lincoln deplored Brown, Lincoln's partner Billy Herndon worshipped Brown. If there was one editor who condemned the raid, there were a half dozen who admired its leader. To Southerners the distinction was elusive or entirely unimportant.

Northern businessmen were foremost in deprecating Harpers Ferry and reassuring the South. Some of them linked their denunciation of Brown with a defense of slavery, however, so that in the logic that usually prevails in time of crisis all critics of Brown risked being smeared with the charge of defending slavery. Radicals called them mossbacks, doughfaces, appeasers, and sought to jeer them out of countenance. "If they cannot be converted, [they] may yet be scared," was Parker's doctrine.

Among the Brown partisans not one has been found but who believed that Harpers Ferry had resulted in great gain for the extremist cause. So profoundly were they convinced of this that they worried little over the conservative dissent. "How vast the change in men's hearts!" exclaimed Phillips. "Insurrection was a harsh, horrid word to millions a month ago." Now it was "the lesson of the hour." Garrison rejoiced that thousands who could not listen to his gentlest rebuke ten years before "now easily

swallow John Brown whole, and his rifle in the bargain."
"They all called him crazy then," wrote Thoreau; "Who
calls him crazy now?" To the poet it seemed that "the
North is suddenly all Transcendentalist." On the day John
Brown was hanged church bells were tolled in com-
memoration in New England towns, out along the Mo-
hawk Valley, in Cleveland and the Western Reserve, in
Chicago and northern Illinois. In Albany one hundred
rounds were fired from a cannon. Writing to his daughter
the following day, Joshua Giddings of Ohio said, "I find
the hatred of slavery greatly intensified by the fate of
Brown and men are ready to march to Virginia and dispose of her despotism at once." It was not long before they
were marching to Virginia, and marching to the tune of
"John Brown's Body."

The Harpers Ferry crisis on the other side of the Potomac was a faithful reflection of the crisis in the North,
and can therefore be quickly sketched. It is the reflection,
with the image reversed in the mirror, that antagonistic
powers present to each other in a war crisis. To the South
John Brown also appeared as a true symbol of Northern
purpose, but instead of the "angel of light" Thoreau pictured, the South saw an angel of destruction. The South
did not seriously question Brown's sanity either, for he
seemed only the rational embodiment of purposes that
Southern extremists had long taught were universal in
the North. The crisis helped propagandists falsely identify
the whole North with John Brownism. For Harpers Ferry

strengthened the hand of extremists and revolutionists in the South as it did in the North, and it likewise discredited and weakened moderates and their influence.

· The risk one runs in describing the reaction to Harpers Ferry is the risk of attributing to that event tendencies long manifest. The South had been living in a crisis atmosphere for a long time. It was a society in the grip of an insecurity complex, a tension resulting from both rational and irrational fears. One cause of it was the steady, invincible expansion of the free-state system in size and power, after the Southern system had reached the limits of its own expansion. The South, therefore, felt itself to be menaced through encirclement by a power containing elements unfriendly to its interests, elements that were growing strong enough to capture the government. The South's insecurity was heightened by having to defend against constant attack an institution it knew to be discredited throughout the civilized world and of which Southerners had once been among the severest critics. Its reaction was to withdraw increasingly from contact with the offending world, to retreat into an isolationism of spirit, and to attempt by curtailing freedom of speech to avoid criticism.

One of the South's tensions sprang from a lack of internal security—the fear of servile insurrection. By the nature of things a slave uprising had to be secret, sudden, and extremely bloody, sparing neither men, women, nor children. The few occurrences of this kind had left a deep trauma in the minds of the people. The pathological character of this tension was manifested in periodic waves of panic based largely on rumor. It is significant that two of the most severe panics of this sort occurred in the election years 1856 and 1860 and were accompanied by charges that abolitionists from the North were fomenting uprisings. Harpers Ferry was therefore a blow at the most sensitive area of Southern consciousness.

The first reaction to the raid, outside Virginia, was surprisingly mild. Newspapers, particularly in the Lower South, pointed out that, after all, the slaves had remained loyal, that Brown's invasion was a complete failure, and that it was quickly suppressed. This mood did not last long, however. The hundreds of captured documents belonging to Brown and his men persuaded Virginia authorities that the conspiracy was widespread and that the Harpers Ferry strike, had it been successful, was intended to be merely the signal for uprisings throughout the South. Among the documents were maps of seven Southern states with certain widely scattered areas and localities marked with symbols. The symbols may have indicated nothing at all, of course, but they were enough to grip the localities concerned with fear.

Another document that inspired terror was a long letter from Lawrence Thatcher (an assumed name), one of Brown's emissaries, reporting two weeks before the raid on a tour of the South. Written from Memphis, the letter suggests the presence of a formidable force of subversives established in the South by Brown's organization. In Tennessee and Arkansas there were reported to be "an immense number of slaves ripe and ready at the very first intimation to strike a decided blow," and the writer was amazed to find "so large a number of whites ready to aid us" in Memphis. A "thorough scouring" of Arkansas convinced him that the readiness of the slaves was such that "a bold stroke of one day will overthrow the whole state." In Brownsville, Tennessee, a subversive white schoolteacher urged that "we must send out more well qualified men to the South as school teachers, and work them in everywhere," that there was "no avocation in which a man can do so much good for our cause" since the people had so much confidence in a schoolteacher. The writer of the letter assured John Brown that "Southern people are easy gulled." His report reveals the man as a wishful thinker and a naïve enthusiast, but after Harpers Ferry, when this letter was found by Virginia authorities, the Southern mind was in no state to distinguish between responsible and irresponsible sources of evidence.

Letters from all parts of the South deluged Governor Wise's mail with reports that Brown conspirators had been seized or punished. These, and the Southern newspapers of the time, portray a society in the throes of panic. Convinced that the South was honeycombed with subversives, Southerners tended to see an abolitionist behind every bush and a slave insurrection brewing in the arrival of any stranger. Victims of vigilante and mob action ranged from aged eccentrics and itinerant piano-tuners to substantial citizens of long residence. The mob spirit was no respecter of person or class. A sixty-year-old minister in Texas, who was a believer in the Biblical sanction of slavery and a Democrat of Kentucky birth, made the mistake of criticizing the treatment of slaves in a sermon and was given seventy lashes on his back. A schoolteacher who had lived in Louisiana and Arkansas for ten years was given thirty-six hours to leave the latter state. The newly arrived president of an Alabama college, who came from New York, was forced to give up his job and flee for his life. In December, 1859, twelve families, including thirty-nine people associated with antislavery schools and churches of Berea, Kentucky, were forcibly expelled from the state for abolitionism.

Southern fire-eaters swore that no Northerner could be trusted and that all should be expelled. Even the humblest workmen from the North were in danger of insult, violence, or lynching. An Irish stonecutter in Columbia, South Carolina, was beaten, tarred and feathered, and expelled from the state by a mob. Three members of the crew of a brig from Maine were brutally flogged in Georgia, and a New England mechanic was driven out of a village in the same state because he was found to have a clean shirt wrapped in a New York paper containing one of Beecher's sermons. Two Connecticut book-peddlers were roughly handled in Charleston when lists of slaves were found in their bags, and two printers were ridden out of Kingstree, South Carolina, on rails. Four men "suspected of being abolition emissaries" were arrested in two days in Columbus, Georgia, and ten peddlers were driven out of the village of Abbeville, Mississippi. Four months after Harpers Ferry a man was lynched in South Carolina as "one of Brown's associates." Not only Northerners but associates of Northerners were subject to persecution, for guilt by association was an accepted principle in the crisis.

Then there was the Southern enemy within the gates to be dealt with. Hinton R. Helper of North Carolina had written an antislavery book, quantities of which were burned in public ceremonies at High Point in his own state, at Greenville, South Carolina, and at Mayesville, Kentucky. Other public book-burning ceremonies took place at Enterprise, Mississippi, and at Montgomery, Alabama, while at Palestine, Texas, the citizens appointed a committee "to collect all said dangerous books for destruction by public burning." Thought control extended to the suppression and seizure of newspapers, a method long practiced, and in Alabama a resolution was introduced in the legislature prohibiting the licensing of teachers with less than ten years' residence, "to protect the state against abolition teachers." Not content with cutting off intellectual commerce with the North, extremists organized to end economic intercourse as well. They published blacklists of Northern firms suspected of abolitionist tendencies, organized boycotts, and promoted nonintercourse agreements. The Richmond *Enquirer* advocated a law "that will keep out of our borders every article of Northern manufacture or importation." On December 8, 1859, thirty-two business agents of New York and Boston arrived in Washington from the South, reporting "indignation so great against Northerners that they were compelled to return and abandon their business."

Southern zealots of secession had no better ally than John Brown. Robert B. Rhett, Edmund Ruffin, and William L. Yancey all rejoiced over the effect of Harpers Ferry. Non-slaveholders saw dramatized before them the menace of a slave uprising and readily concluded that their wives and children, as much as the home of the planter, were threatened with the horror of insurrection. They frequently became more fanatical secessionists than the planters. In face of the Northern apotheosis of Brown there was little that Southern moderates could say in answer to such pronouncements as that of the New Orleans *Picayune* of December 2: "Crime becomes godliness, and criminals, red from the slaughter of innocent, are exalted to eminence beside the divine gospel of Peace." The Charleston *Mercury* of November 29 rejoiced that Harpers Ferry, "like a slap in the face," had roused Virginia from her hesitant neutrality and started her on the road to secession. "I have never before seen the public mind of Va. so deeply moved," wrote a Virginian sadly. "The people are far in advance of the politicians, and would most cheerfully follow the extremist counsels. Volunteer companies, horse & foot, are springing up everywhere."

The crisis psychology of 1859 persisted and deepened in the fateful year of 1860 into a pathological condition of mind in which delusions of persecution and impending disaster flourished. Out of Texas came wild rumors of incendiary fires, abolitionists plotting with slaves, and impending insurrection on a vast scale. Rumors of large stocks of strychnine in the possession of slaves and of plans for well-poisoning were widely believed, though unproved. One scholar has aptly compared the tension of the South in 1860 with the "Great Fear" that seized the rural provinces of France in the summer of 1789 when panic spread the word that "the brigands are coming." In that atmosphere the South made the momentous decision that split the Democratic Party at Charleston in April, and before the mood was gone it was debating secession.

In the course of the crisis each of the antagonists, according to the immemorial pattern, had become convinced of the depravity and diabolism of the other. Each believed itself persecuted, menaced. "Let the 'higher law' of abolitionism be met by the 'higher law' of self-preservation," demanded the Richmond *Enquirer*. Lynch law was the only answer to pikes. "What additional insults and outrages *will* arouse it [the North] to assert its rights?" demanded Garrison. And Garrison's opposite number in Mississippi, Albert Gallatin Brown, cried: "Oh, God! To what depths of infamy are we sinking in the South if we allow these things to pass." Paranoia continued to induce counterparanoia, each antagonist infecting the other reciprocally, until the vicious spiral ended in war.

4

Equality: The Deferred Commitment

NOW THAT THE DRIVE IS ON TO GIVE ACCUSTOMED CANT about equality for the Negro some basis in fact and to deliver on promises nearly a century old, the temptation is strong to pretend that we have been in earnest all along. Such a pretense, successfully maintained, might stiffen resolution, put the forces of resistance further on the defensive, and in general further a good cause. Before we become so deeply committed to the pretense that we believe in it ourselves, however, it would be well to look soberly into the curious origins of the commitment to equality during the Civil War and into its subsequent abandonment.

The North had a much more difficult time defining its war aims than the South. The aims of the South were fixed and obvious from the start and remained constant until rendered hopeless—the establishment and defense of independence. The North moved gradually and gropingly toward a definition of its war aims. Its progress was obstructed by doubt and misgiving and characterized by much backing and filling. The debate and the outcome were shaped by the course of the war itself, by military necessities, foreign propaganda needs, and domestic morale demands, as well as by the exigencies of party politics and political ambitions.

As the North progressed toward the framing of war objectives, America was inched along from right to left. It moved from hesitant support of a limited war with essentially negative aims toward a total war with positive and revolutionary aims. The character of the war changed from a pragmatic struggle for power to a crusade for ideals. The struggle took on many aspects of an ideological war, and in some minds became a holy war, fought, financed, and supported by men who could feel themselves instruments of divine will.

It was far different at the outset. Lincoln was inaugurated President of a slaveholding republic. He had been elected on a platform firmly pledging him to the protection of the institution of slavery where it existed, and in his first inaugural address, while not abandoning his moral views of slavery, he explicitly denied that he entertained any "purpose, directly or indirectly, to interfere with the institution of slavery in the states where it exists." Not only had he no purpose, but he declared he had "no lawful right" and indeed, "no inclination to do so." He assured the people of the South that their property was not "in any wise endangered by the now incoming administration." His emphasis was upon the negative aim of preventing secession and the disruption of the Union.

Four and a half months later, after blood had been shed

and the war was in full swing, Congress took a hand in defining war aims. On July 22 the House adopted, with only two negative votes, a resolution declaring that "this war is not waged . . . [for the] purpose of overthrowing or interfering with the . . . established institutions of those States, but to . . . maintain . . . the . . . States unimpaired; and that as soon as these objects are accomplished the war ought to cease." The Senate backed this sentiment up with a similar resolution, also adopted by a nearly unanimous vote. At this stage, so far as both President and Congress were able to formulate war aims, this was a war of narrowly limited objectives and no revolutionary purpose. It was to be a war against secession, a war to maintain the Union—that, and nothing more.

This negative phase did not last long. No mood lasted very long in the flux and change of the Civil War. Five months later the House voted down a motion to reaffirm the resolution of limited war aims. Already the movement was under way to extend those aims from mere Union to embrace freedom as well. The second war aim was not attained by a stroke of Lincoln's pen, as Lincoln was the first to admit. It was forced by events, by necessities, and those events and necessities first took the shape of thousands of pitiable fugitive slaves crowding into the Union lines. Their path toward freedom was tedious and rugged, filled with obstacles. Thousands wavered between freedom and slavery for years and were never quite sure when freedom came, or if it did. The majority only began their struggle for freedom after the war was over.

Freedom as a war aim was arrived at by a long succession of piecemeal decisions. There were orders by field commanders, some countermanded, some sustained; there were acts of state legislatures; and there was a long succession of bits and driblets of emancipation enacted by Congress, which did not get around to repealing the Fugitive Slave Act until June of 1864. And always there was the embarrassed and reluctant dragon of emancipation, the invading army. "Although war has not been waged against slavery," wrote Secretary Seward to Charles Francis Adams in 1862, "yet the army acts . . . as an emancipating crusade. To proclaim the crusade is unnecessary."

The crusade *was* eventually proclaimed, though the proclamation was not the President's. Lincoln never wanted to turn the war into a moral crusade. It is not necessary to retrace here the painful steps by which Lincoln arrived at his numerous decisions upon slavery and emancipation. It is sometimes forgotten, however, how often he deprecated the importance of his Proclamation of Emancipation. He characterized it as a war necessity, forced by events, ineffectual, inadequate, and of doubtful legality. It is plain that his heart was in his plan for gradual emancipation, which he repeatedly but unsuccessfully urged upon Congress and proposed as a Constitutional amendment. This was an extremely conservative plan for gradual and voluntary emancipation over a period of thirty-seven years, to be completed by 1900, to be administered by the slave states themselves, and to be assisted by the Federal government with compensation to slaveowners and foreign colonization of freedmen. Support was not forthcoming, and war developments underlined the impracticality of the plan.

When Lincoln finally resorted to the Proclamation, he presented it as a war measure, authorized by war powers and justified by military necessity. Again and again he repeated that it was a means to an end—the limited Lincolnian end of union—and not an end in itself, that union and not freedom was the true war aim. Yet freedom had become a second war aim anyway, and for many the primary war aim. In spite of the fact that the Proclamation emancipated no slaves, it had a profound effect upon the war—more effect upon the war, in fact, than upon slavery.

For one thing, it helped to elevate the war to a new plane. It was still a war for union, but not as before—a war for union with slavery. It was no longer merely a war against something, but a war for something, a war for something greatly cherished in American tradition and creed, a war for freedom. What had started as a war for political ends had, by virtue of military necessity, undergone a metamorphosis into a higher and finer thing, a war for moral ends. What had commenced as a police action had been converted into a crusade. Some abolitionists professed disappointment in the Proclamation, but so ardent a believer as Theodore Tilton was in "a bewilderment of joy" with the new spirit "so racing up and down and through my blood that I am half crazy with enthusiasm."

The great majority of citizens in the North still abhorred any association with abolitionists, but any of them were now free to share the forbidden transports of the despised radicals at no cost to their reputation whatever. Conservative, humdrum, unheroic millions could now sing "John Brown's Body" in naïve identification with the demented old hero and partake, vicariously and quite inexpensively, of his martyrdom. An aura of glory descended upon the common cause that sometimes lifted men out of themselves, exalted them, though it seems to have inspired civilians and noncombatants more often than soldiers. It could endow men with a sense of moral superiority and divine purpose that enabled them to regard the enemy with a new indignation and righteousness. It emboldened them to make messianic pronouncements with no apparent self-consciousness. The exuberant religiosity of the age was tapped for war propaganda and yielded riches. How otherwise could men, with no consciousness of blasphemy, lift their voices to sing, "As He died to make men holy, let us die to make men free"?

Before he issued the proclamation, Lincoln had written privately that he was holding the antislavery pressure "within bounds." He could no longer make that boast with assurance, for after the edict of January 1, 1863, antislavery sentiment could not always be kept in bounds. As Professor James G. Randall put it, "The concomitants of emancipation got out of Lincoln's hands. He could issue his proclamation, but he could not control the radicals." The "concomitant" of the second war aim of freedom was a third—equality. No sooner was the Union officially committed to the second war aim than the drive was on for commitment to the third.

It cannot be said that this drive was as successful as the

movement for freedom, nor that by the end of the war the country was committed to equality in the same degree it was to freedom. There was no Equality Proclamation to match the Emancipation Proclamation. The third war aim never gained from Lincoln even the qualified support he gave to abolition. Without presidential blessing the commitment was eventually made, made piecemeal like that to freedom, and with full implications not spelled out until after the war—but it was made.

The formal commitment to the third war aim would never have been possible had the abolitionist minority not been able to appeal to more venerable and acceptable doctrine than their own. It would be preposterous to credit the abolitionists with surreptitiously introducing the idea of equality into America. The nation was born with the word on its tongue. The first of those "self-evident" truths of the Declaration was that "all men are created equal." Back of that was the heritage of natural rights doctrine, and back of that the great body of Christian dogma and the teaching that all men are equal in the sight of God.

There were, of course, less disinterested inducements in operation. If freedom was in part a military expedient, equality was in part a political and economic expedient. Equality of the franchise for freedmen was deemed essential to Republican supremacy, and Republican supremacy was considered necessary by influential classes to protect the new economic order.

Equality was advisable, not only politically and economically, but also from a psychological and religious standpoint. For fulfillment of abolitionist purposes it was almost a necessity. Abolitionists had grounded their whole crusade against slavery on the proposition that it was a "sin." It is not sufficient simply to abolish a sin; it has to be expiated, and the sinner purified. Purification and expiation involve penance and suffering. Equality had a punitive purpose: the infliction of a penance of humiliation upon the status of the sinner. For those with an uncomplicated interest in sheer vengeance upon a hated foe, equality had punitive uses of a simpler sort.

Even with all these resources at their command, however, the radicals could never have succeeded in their drive for the formal commitment to equality had it not been launched upon the mounting tide of war spirit and had the war not already been converted into a moral crusade. A moral crusade could only be justified by high moral aims, even if those aims were embraced by the great majority as an afterthought, by many with important mental reservations, and by others as expedients for extraneous ends having nothing whatever to do with the welfare of the freedmen.

So far as the abolitionist minority was concerned, the association of freedom and equality, as Jacobus tenBroek has demonstrated, was rooted in three decades of organized antislavery agitation. Antislavery congressmen carried this association of aims into the framing of the Thirteenth Amendment. Debates over the question in the Senate in the spring of 1864 and in the House of Representatives in January, 1865, contain evidence that the framers aimed at equality as well as emancipation. Both objectives were assumed by the opponents as well as the sponsors of the amendment during the debate. As one of the supporters, William D. Kelley of Pennsylvania, put it: "The proposed Amendment is designed . . . to accomplish . . . the abolition of slavery in the United States, and the political and social elevation of Negroes to all the rights of white men." His broad construction of the amendment was echoed with variations by numerous supporters. They did not include enfranchisement among the rights of Negroes, but they specifically and repeatedly mentioned equal protection of the laws, safeguard for privileges and immunities, and guarantee against deprivation of life, liberty, and property without due process of law. The main ground of opposition to the amendment was this very aim of equality. A constant complaint of opponents was that the amendment would not only free the Negroes but would "make them our equals before the law."

The broad construction of the Thirteenth Amendment to include equality as well as freedom was not sustained when put to test, and the radicals themselves abandoned the interpretation. But they did not abandon their aim of equality. Instead, they increased the scope of it. Responding to provocation of Southern aggression against Negro rights and to inducement of political gains as well, they proceeded to make equality as much the law of the land as freedom. In the Civil Rights Act of 1866 they gave sweeping protection to the rights of Negroes as citizens, guaranteeing them "full and equal benefit of all laws and proceedings for security of person and property, as is enjoyed by white citizens," regardless of any law to the contrary. When the President vetoed the bill, they passed it over his veto. When doubt was cast upon its constitutionality, they enacted most of its provisions into the Fourteenth Amendment. When the South balked at ratification, they stipulated its adoption as a condition of readmission to the Union. Later they extended Federal protection to the Negro franchise by the Fifteenth Amendment. They re-enacted the Civil Rights Act, implementing protection of voters, and followed that by another bill to carry out rights established by the Fourteenth Amendment. To crown the achievement they passed still another Civil Rights Act in 1875 which provided sweepingly that "all persons within the jurisdiction of the United States shall be entitled to the full and equal enjoyment of the accommodations, advantages, facilities, and privileges of inns, public conveyances on land or water, theatres, and other places of public amusement, subject only to the conditions and limitations established by law and applicable alike to citizens of every race and color, regardless of any previous condition of servitude."

Thus, by every device of emphasis, repetition, re-enactment, and reiteration, the radical lawmakers and Constitution-amenders would seem to have nailed down all loose ends, banished all ambiguity, and left no doubt whatever about their intention to extend Federal protection to Negro equality. So far as it was humanly possible to do so by statute and constitutional amendment, America would seem to have been firmly committed to the principle of equality.

And yet we know that within a very short time after

these imposing commitments were made they were broken. America reneged, shrugged off the obligation, and all but forgot about it for nearly a century. The commitments to the war aims of union and freedom were duly honored, but not the third commitment. In view of current concern over the default and belated effort to make amends, it might be of interest to inquire how and why it ever occurred.

Equality was a far more revolutionary aim than freedom, though it may not have seemed so at first. Slavery seemed so formidable, so powerfully entrenched in law and property, and so fiercely defended by arms that it appeared far the greater obstacle. Yet slavery was property based on law. The law could be changed and the property expropriated. Not so inequality. Its entrenchments were deeper and subtler. The attainment of equality involved many more relationships than those between master and slave. It was a revolution that was not confined to the boundaries of the defeated and discredited South, as emancipation largely was. It was a revolution for the North as well. It involved such unpredictable and biased people as hotel clerks, railroad conductors, steamboat stewards, theater ushers, real estate agents, and policemen. In fact, it could involve almost anybody. It was clear from the start that this revolution was going to require enthusiastic and widespread support in the North to make it work.

Was there any such support? Who were the American people so firmly committed to this revolutionary change, and what degree of support were they prepared to lend it? For one thing, among the Union-supporting people were those of the border area, which included not only Kentucky, Missouri, and West Virginia but also the Southern parts of Ohio, Indiana, and Illinois. This area embraced a white population approximately equal to the number of whites in the Confederate states. And if Maryland be added, as I think it should be, that area included considerably more white people than the Confederacy. Most of those people were still living in slave states during the war, and many of their attitudes and habits were not very different from those of people in states to the southward. Their enthusiasm for the third war aim was a matter of some doubt.

What of the Republican party itself, the party responsible for enacting the commitment to equality? During the war it was, of course, exclusively a sectional party, a party of Northern people. Its membership was heavily recruited from the defunct Whig party, and the new party never shook off its Whiggish origins. Many of its members, to use Lincoln's phrase, disliked being "unwhigged." The essence of Whiggery was accommodation and compromise, compromise of many kinds, including the old type of sectional compromise. Before Reconstruction was over, Republicans were again seeking out their old Whig friends of the South with proffered compromise that would leave the solution of the race question in Southern hands.

Lincoln was fully aware of the limited moral resources of his party and his section of the country. He knew that there were limits beyond which popular conviction and conscience could not be pushed in his time. Whatever his personal convictions—and he may, as one historian has maintained, have been entirely color blind—when he spoke as President of the United States or as leader of his political party, he spoke with measured words. And he did not speak in one way to Negroes and another to whites. To a delegation of Negro leaders at the White House he said, "There is an unwillingness on the part of our people, harsh as it may be, for you free colored people to remain with us." He expressed deep sympathy for their wrongs as slaves. "But even when you cease to be slaves," he said, "you are yet far removed from being placed on an equality with the white race. . . . The aspiration of men is to enjoy equality with the best when free, but on this broad continent not a single man of your race is made the equal of a single man of ours. . . . I cannot alter it if I would. It is a fact. . . . It is better for us both, therefore, to be separated." This idea of separating the races led Lincoln to support the most impractical and illusory plan of his entire career, the plan for colonizing the freedmen abroad or settling them in segregated colonies at home.

What were the sentiments of the Federal Army—the army of liberation—about the issue of equality? That great body included eventually more than two million men. There appears to have been a lower proportion of men from the upper income and social classes, and a higher proportion of the lower economic and social order in the Federal than in the Confederate Army. But there were men of all kinds and all views. Among them were officers and enlisted men of deep and abiding conviction, dedicated spirits whose devotion to the moral aims of the war is borne out in their conduct and in their treatment of slaves, freedmen, and Negro soldiers.

Unfortunately it cannot be said that soldiers of this turn of mind were typical of the army sentiment, or even that they were very numerous. They seem, on the contrary, to have been quite untypical. "One who reads letters and diaries of Union soldiers," writes Professor Bell I. Wiley, who has indeed read many of them, "encounters an enormous amount of antipathy toward Negroes. Expressions of unfriendliness range from blunt statements bespeaking intense hatred to belittling remarks concerning dress and demeanor." Many of the Union soldiers brought their race prejudices with them from civilian life. Sometimes these prejudices were mitigated by contact with the Negro, but more often they appear to have been intensified and augmented by army experience. Men who endure the hardships and suffering and boredom of war have always sought scapegoats on which to heap their miseries. In the Civil War the Negroes who crowded into Union lines were made to order for the role of scapegoat. The treatment they often received at the hands of their liberators makes some of the darkest pages of war history. Another shameful chapter is the treatment of the 200,000 Negroes who served in the Union Army. Enlistment of Negroes in the first place appears to have been strongly opposed by the great majority of white troops. And even after their battle record proved, as Dudley T. Cornish says, "that Negro soldiers measured up to the standard set for American soldiers generally," they continued to be discriminated against by unequal pay, allowances, and opportunities. These inequalities lasted throughout the war. It would seem at times that the army of liberation marched southward on its crusade under the banner of White Supremacy.

One is driven by the evidence to the conclusion that the radicals committed the country to a guarantee of equality that popular convictions were not prepared to sustain, that legal commitments overreached moral persuasion. The lag between conviction and commitment could be illustrated by many more examples, including race riots and violent labor demonstrations against the Negro that broke out during the war in Cleveland, Cincinnati, Chicago, Detroit, Buffalo, Albany, Brooklyn and New York. The tendency would also be revealed by the neglect, exclusion, or hostility that craft unions and national unions exhibited toward the Negro during the war years and afterward. Further illustration could be drawn from the measures adopted by Western states to discourage freedmen from settling or working within their boundaries, or going to school with their children. One should also recall that in all but a handful of Northern states suffrage was denied the Negro long after it was mandatory for freedmen in the South.

In concentrating on the North as a source of illustration of this moral lag on equality, I have certainly not intended to suggest that it was peculiar to the North. I have taken agreement for granted that the lag was even greater in the South and that resistance to fulfillment of the commitment was in that area even more widespread, stubborn, and effective. It *has* been my intention, however, to suggest that the default was not peculiar to the South.

When such a lag develops between popular convictions and constitutional commitments, and when that lapse cannot be conveniently rationalized by statutory or amendatory procedures, it becomes the embarrassing task of the Supreme Court of the United States to square ideals with practice, to effect a rationalization. The justices in this instance examined the words of the Fourteenth Amendment and, by what Justice John M. Harlan in a famous dissenting opinion called "subtle and ingenious verbal criticism," discovered that they did not at all mean what they seemed to mean, nor what their authors thought they meant. By a series of opinions beginning in 1873 the court constricted the Fourteenth Amendment by a narrow interpretation which proclaimed that privileges and immunities we call civil rights were not placed under federal protection at all. In effect, they found that the commitment to equality had never really been made.

The Union fought the Civil War on borrowed moral capital. With their noble belief in their purpose and their extravagant faith in the future, the radicals ran up a staggering war debt, a moral debt that was soon found to be beyond the country's capacity to pay, given the undeveloped state of its moral resources at the time. After making a few token payments during Reconstruction, the United States defaulted on the debt and unilaterally declared a moratorium that lasted more than eight decades. The country was only nominally spared the formality of bankruptcy by the injunctions of the Supreme Court that cast doubt on the validity of the debt. In the meantime, over the years, interest on the debt accumulated. The debt was further augmented by the shabby treatment of the forgotten creditors, our own Negro citizens.

Then in the middle of the twentieth century conscience finally began to catch up with commitment. Very suddenly, relatively speaking, it became clear that the almost forgotten Civil War debt had to be paid, paid in full, and without any more stalling than was necessary. As in the case of the commitment to emancipation during the Civil War, amoral forces and pressures such as the exigencies of foreign propaganda, power politics, and military necessities exercised a powerful influence upon the recommitment to equality. But also as in the case of emancipation, the voices of conscience, of national creed, and of religious conviction played their parts. In the second instance the demands of the Negroes themselves played a more important part in the pressure than before. Equality was at last an idea whose time, long deferred, had finally come.

Once again there was a lag between popular conviction and constitutional interpretation. Only this time the trend ran the opposite way, and it was the Constitution that dawdled behind conviction. Again it proved unfeasible to close the gap by statutory or amendatory procedures, and again it became the embarrassing task of the Supreme Court to effect an accommodation, a rationalization. Once more the justices scrutinized the words of the Fourteenth Amendment, and this time they discovered that those words really meant what they said, and presumably had all along. The old debt that the court had once declared invalid they now pronounced valid.

Although this was acknowledged to be a national debt,

in the nature of things it would have to be paid by a special levy that fell with disproportionate heaviness upon one section of the country. The South had been called on before to bear the brunt of a guilty national conscience. It is now called on a second time. One could hope that the South's experience in these matters might stand it in good stead, that having learned to swallow its own words before, it might do so again with better grace, that it might perform what is required of it with forbearance and humility. I do not know. I can only admit that present indications are not very reassuring.

There is no apparent prospect of full compliance nor of an easy solution. The white South is resisting, and a reactionary part of it is defiant. The resistance is stubborn. A minority could become nasty and its defiance brutish. Already there is evidence that the patience of the rest of the country is not unlimited. There is a sense of frustration and a demand that there be no more faltering. The taunts and jeers of our foreign adversaries are a provocation, and so are the partisan rivalries of politicians. The demand for stern measures and the use of armed force is growing. An example has already been set and more could follow. But the center of resistance has scarcely been seriously challenged, and when it is, the prospect is likely to grow even darker. These are facts that no one can contemplate soberly without a sense of foreboding.

We are presently approaching the centennial anniversary of the Civil War. Simultaneously we are approaching the climax of a new sectional crisis—a crisis that divides the country along much the same old sectional lines, over many of the same old sectional issues. It would be an ironic, not to say tragic, coincidence if the celebration of the anniversary took place in the midst of a crisis reminiscent of the one celebrated.

The historian who, in these circumstances, writes the commemorative volumes for the Civil War centennial would seem to have a special obligation of sobriety and fidelity to the record. If he writes in that spirit, he will flatter the self-righteousness of neither side. He will not picture the North as burning for equality since 1863 with a hard, gem-like flame. He will not picture the South as fighting for the eternal verities. He will not paint a holy war that ennobled its participants. And he will try to keep in mind the humility that prevented the central figure in the drama from ever falling in with the notion that he was the incarnation of the Archangel Michael.

———

Postscript, 1968: In the foregoing pages numerous doubts were raised about the depth and extent of the original Republican commitment to racial equality. Further research since this essay was written has raised more doubts, especially about support for equality in the Middle West and among certain Eastern Radicals. Additional investigation has also disclosed more ambiguity than originally appeared in the Federal laws and Constitutional amendments extending protection to Negro equality. These findings are reported in the author's "Seeds of Failure in Radical Race Policy," in *Proceedings of the American Philosophical Society,* CX (February, 1966), 1–9.

For an assessment of the anticipations of Southern and Northern reactions written in the early phases of the Second Reconstruction, see the essay "What Happened to the Civil Rights Movement," pp. 167–86, added in this revision and written in the hindsight and from the vantage point provided by another post-Reconstruction era.

5

The Political Legacy of the
First Reconstruction

OF ALL THE REVOLUTIONARY PROPOSALS THAT EVENTUALLY
received the sanction of law in the upheaval of Reconstruction, the proposal to give the freedmen the unre-
stricted right to vote was one of the most difficult for contemporaries to accept, in the North as well as in the South.
Emancipation itself had been repeatedly disavowed as a
war aim until the war was well under way. Civil rights for
freedmen was another cautiously advanced afterthought.
Enfranchisement came in belatedly, surreptitiously, almost
disingenuously advanced by its proponents, grudgingly accepted by a North that moved under duress and the argument of necessity and greeted with gloomy forebodings
of failure, if not disaster. These attitudes were widespread,
and they were not confined to copperheads, doughfaces,
and mossback conservatives.

Representative of the skeptical and negative attitude of
the time is the following pronouncement: "When was it
ever known that liberation from bondage was accompanied by a recognition of political equality? Chattels per-

sonal may be instantly translated from the auction-block into freemen; but when were they ever taken at the same time to the ballot-box, and invested with all political rights and immunities? According to the laws of development and progress, it is not practicable. . . . Nor, if the freed blacks were admitted to the polls by Presidential fiat, do I see any permanent advantage likely to be secured by it; for, submitted to as a necessity at the outset, as soon as the state was organized and left to manage its own affairs, the white population, with their superior intelligence, wealth, and power, would unquestionably alter the franchise in accordance with their prejudices, and exclude those thus summarily brought to the polls. Coercion would gain nothing."

The author of these sentiments, written in 1864, was none other than William Lloyd Garrison of the *Liberator,* the man who swore to be "harsh as truth and uncompromising as justice." Nor was he alone among the abolitionists in these sentiments, for the radicals themselves were divided on the matter of Negro suffrage. Even Senator Charles Sumner, one of the earlier and most powerful advocates of placing the ballot in the freedman's hands, was prepared in a Senate speech on February 5, 1866, to admit that educational qualifications for the suffrage would be advisable. At that time, of course, educational restrictions, even a literacy test fairly administered, would have limited the franchise to a small minority of the freedmen. Horace Greeley of the New York *Tribune,* an old friend of the slave, would "limit the voting privilege to the competent and deserving" and suggested such qualifications as ability to read and write, payment of taxes, or establishment in a trade. General O. O. Howard, head of the Freedmen's Bureau, hoped that the franchise would be limited "at least by an educational qualification." This far, of course, President Lincoln and President Johnson were prepared to go, and both in fact did unsuccessfully recommend to Southern states such franchise laws.

To go further than that in 1866 or even later was to incur grave political risks, that even the most radical of Republicans were reluctant to assume. Only five states in the North, all with a negligible percentage of colored population, provided for Negro franchise. In 1865 Wisconsin, Minnesota, and Connecticut defeated proposals to allow the Negroes to vote, and the Nebraska constitution of 1866 confined suffrage to whites. New Jersey and Ohio in 1867 and Michigan and Pennsylvania in 1868 turned down proposals for Negro suffrage. Dr. W. E. B. Du Bois, who contends that in 1861 "probably not one white American in a hundred believed that Negroes could become an integral part of American democracy," concludes that even by 1868 "the country was not ready for Negro suffrage."

Yet Negro suffrage did come. It came very quickly. In fact, by 1868 it had already come in the South. How it came and why are important determinants in the political legacy left the South and the American Negro by Reconstruction.

Thaddeus Stevens, foremost champion of the freedmen, master of the Republican House majority, and leader of Radical Reconstruction, was advocating some extremely radical measures. He was quite ready to disfranchise Southern whites in great numbers and to confiscate great quantities of their land. "It is intended to revolutionize their feelings and principles," he declared. "This may startle feeble minds and shake weak nerves. So do all great improvements." To those who objected to humiliating the defeated foe, he replied: "Why not? Do not they deserve humiliation? If they do not, who does? What criminal, what felon deserves it more?"

But for all his radicalism, Stevens was not yet prepared to enfranchise the Negro freedmen. For one thing, of course, he knew that public opinion would not support it and that the majority of his own party was against it. But apart from political reasons he had other doubts about the wisdom of the measure, some of them similar to those expressed by Garrison, Greeley, Howard, and, for that matter, President Andrew Johnson.

On this vital matter Stevens, contrary to his reputation, can be classified as a moderate or conservative. For one thing he doubted that the freedmen were prepared for intelligent voting. The conditions and laws of slavery, he said on December 18, 1865, "have prevented them from acquiring an education, understanding the commonest laws of contract, or of managing the ordinary business of life." The following month, on January 31, 1866, while urging a constitutional amendment basing representation in the House on the number of qualified voters in a state, Stevens actually expressed hope that the Southern states would not immediately grant the freedmen suffrage and thereby increase Southern voting power in Congress. He assumed that the Negroes would fall under the political influence of their former masters. "I do not therefore want to grant them this privilege for some years . . . four or five years hence, when the freedmen shall have been made free indeed, when they shall have become intelligent enough, and there are sufficient loyal men there to control the representation from those States," Negro voting would be safe enough. In fact, at this time, Stevens adopted a states' rights position: "I hold that the States have the right, and always have had it, to fix the elective franchise within their own States."

Stevens' solution to the freedmen's suffrage problem was to force upon the Southern states the dilemma posed by the proposed Fourteenth Amendment. According to these terms the states would have to choose between excluding the freedmen from the ballot box, thus reducing their number of representatives to about forty-six, or on the other hand, enfranchising them, thereby increasing their representatives to about eighty-three but running the grave risk of losing control to the Republican party. To ensure the adoption of the amendment Stevens proposed that it be submitted only to the non-Southern states and declared adopted when approved by three-fourths of these states, exclusive of the South. This solution was rejected by his party, and the Southern states voted the amendment down when it was submitted to them along with the other states.

Still hesitant, still reluctant to accept immediate freedman's suffrage and impose it by force, Stevens temporized with still another proposal. This was contained in a bill he introduced on December 13, 1866, for the reconstruction of North Carolina. In this he proposed to restrict the ballot to those of both races who could read and write or who owned real estate assessed at a value of a hundred dollars or more. Loyal men who had voted before (whites) were not to be disfranchised, but certain classes of Confederates were. There was at times, as Ralph Korngold has suggested, something of Lincoln's hesitant approach to emancipation about Stevens' approach to enfranchisement. Hesitation ceased, however, early in 1867, almost two years after the war. He now went the whole way of military rule, disfranchisement of large numbers of Southern whites and immediate and universal Negro suffrage—full scale Radical Reconstruction.

Reasons for the conversion of Thaddeus Stevens will always be debated. A few facts stand out, however, with inescapable clarity. President Johnson's plan of reconstruction would have increased the Southern delegation in the House of Representatives by some thirteen members, since all the freedmen instead of three-fifths would have been counted in apportionment. Without Negro ballots it was probable that all the additional seats, plus all the rest of the seats of the eleven states, would be filled by Democrats and not Republicans. These same states would not only swell the opposition votes in Congress but the electoral votes in presidential contests. About thirty-seven of the Southern seats in the House would be accounted for by Negro population, who had no votes, and likely filled by sworn opponents of the party that took credit for Negro freedom. To ask an overwhelmingly Republican Congress —radical or conservative—to approve such a plan was to ask water to run uphill. Conservative Republicans were no more ready to commit political hara-kiri than Radical Republicans.

"Another good reason is," said Stevens in support of his plan, "it would insure the ascendancy of the Union [Republican] party. Do you avow the party purpose? exclaims some horror stricken demagogue. I do. For I believe, on my conscience, that on the continued ascendancy of that party depends the safety of this great nation. If impartial [Negro] suffrage is excluded in the rebel States then every one of them is sure to send a solid rebel [Democratic] representation to Congress, and cast a solid rebel electoral vote. They, with their kindred Copperheads [Democrats] of the North, would always elect the President and control Congress."

Stevens' follower, Roscoe Conkling of New York, was quite as blunt and more specific. "Shall one hundred and twenty-seven thousand white people in New York cast but one vote in this House and have but one voice here, while the same number of white people in Mississippi have three votes in three voices? Shall the death of slavery add two fifths to the entire power which slavery had when slavery was living? Shall one white man have as much share in the Government as three other white men merely because he lives where blacks out-number whites two to one? . . . No sir; not if I can help it."

In addition to "the party purpose" so frankly avowed by Stevens, there was another purpose which was not frankly declared. It was more often disavowed, concealed, deprecated. This was the purpose of the business community. Although there were significant divisions within the community, a powerful group saw in the return of a disaffected and Democratic South a menace to the economic order that had been established during the absence of the seceding states from the Union. On nearly every delicate and disturbing economic issue of the day—taxation, the National Bank, the national debt, government bonds and their funding, railroads and their financing, regulation of corporations, government grants and subsidies to business, protective tariff legislation—on one and all the business community recognized in the unreconstructed South an antagonist of long standing. In combination with traditional allies in the West and North, the South could upset the new order. Under these circumstances, the Northern business community, except for the banking and mercantile interests allied with the Democrats, put aside conservative habits and politics and threw its support to Radical Reconstruction.

Neither the party purpose, the business purpose, nor the two combined constituted a reputable justification with which to persuade the public to support a radical and unpopular program. But there was a purpose that *was* both reputable and persuasive—the philanthropic purpose, the argument that the freedmen needed the ballot to defend and protect their dearly bought freedom, their newly won civil rights, their welfare and livelihood. Of their philanthropic argument the Radicals could make a persuasive and cogent case. And it is undoubtedly true that some of the Radicals were motivated almost entirely by their idealism and their genuine concern for the rights and welfare of the freedmen. What is doubtful is that these were the effective or primary motives, or that they took priority over the pragmatic and materialistic motives of party advantage and sectional economic interests. It is clear at any rate that, until the latter were aroused and marshaled, the former made little progress. On the whole the skepticism of Secretary Gideon Welles would seem to be justified. "It is evident," he wrote in his diary, "that intense partisanship instead of philanthropy is the root of the movement."

This ulterior motivation, then, is the incubus with which the Negro was burdened before he was ever awakened into political life. The operative and effective motives of his political genesis were extraneous to his own interests and calculated to serve other ends. If there ever came a time when those ends—party advantage and sectional business interests—were better served in some other way, even in a way destructive of the basic political rights of the race, then the political prospects of the Negro would darken. Another incubus was the strongly partisan identifications of his political origins. The major national party of opposition took no part in those origins, regarded them as wholly inimical to its interests, and consequently felt no real commitment to the movement nor to the preservation of its fruits. If there came a time when that party was in the ascendancy, even locally, the political future of the Negro again would darken. To these evil portents should be added the strong resistance to Negro suffrage in the Northern states, the obvious reluctance and hesitance of radical leaders to commit the party to that course, and the grudging acquiescence of the North in the coercive use of it in the South.

After enfranchisement was in full effect in the Southern states, the Republican party felt obliged to give specific promise to the people of the North that they would be left free to keep the Negro disfranchised in their own states. In the Republican platform of 1868 appeared the following: "The guaranty by Congress of equal suffrage to all loyal men at the South was demanded by every consideration of public safety, of gratitude, and of justice, and must be maintained; while the question of suffrage in all loyal [non-Southern] States properly belongs to the people of those States." Only after the presidential election was over and General Grant had won did the party dare bring forward the Fifteenth Amendment denying the right of any state to disfranchise the Negro, and not until 1870 was its ratification completed.

In the meantime a political revolution was under way in the Southern states, a revolution that is the first chapter in the history of the Negro voter in America. The initial step under military government, after the destruction of the old civil governments, was the creation of the new electorate in 1867 and 1868. In all, more than 703,000 Negroes and some 627,000 whites were registered as qualified voters in the reconstructed states. The processes of disfranchisement and enfranchisement were going on simultaneously. The number of whites disfranchised is unknown and unknowable, but it is evident from a comparison of population and registration figures that the number was rather large in some states. While only two states had a colored majority of population, five states were given a colored majority of registered voters. The male population of voting age in Louisiana in 1860 was 94,711 whites and 92,502 Negroes, but only 45,218 whites were registered as against 84,436 Negroes. Alabama's voting age population in 1860 was 113,871 whites and 92,404 Negroes, but only 61,295 whites were registered against 104,518 Negroes. While some states with white majorities in population were given colored majorities in their electorate, others had their white majorities drastically reduced, and the two states with a preponderance of Negroes in population, South Carolina and Mississippi, had overwhelming majorities of colored voters.

This new-born electorate of freedmen was plunged immediately into action by the election of delegates to constitutional conventions. They followed by electing legislative bodies, state and local officials, and by full-scale and continuous participation in all phases and aspects of political life in a period that was abnormally active in a political way. To characterize the quality of the performance of this many people over a decade of time and in a multiplicity of activities with sweeping adjectives, "good" or "bad" or "indifferent," would be to indulge in empty generalities. That the mass of these people had less education, less experience in public affairs, and less property of all sorts than the white voters is obvious. As for the more intangible endowments of status and inner security that the psychologists stress, their relative impoverishment was appalling, unprecedented among American or any other known electorates. Their very appearance at the polls in mass, wearing the rags of slave days and bearing the ancient stigmata of oppression, conjured up every gloomy prognostication of the fate of democracies from Aristotle to the Federalists. Not Athens, nor Rome, nor Paris at greatest turbulence had confronted their like. Here was the Federalist beast who would turn every garden into a pigsty. Here was old John Adams' shiftless and improvident Demos, pawn of demagogues and plutocrats and menace to all order. Here in the flesh was Hamilton's "turbulent and changing" mass who "seldom judge or determine right" and who made it necessary to give to "the rich and well born" that "distinct, permanent share in the government," which alone would insure stability. Here was the ultimate test of the democratic dogma in the most extreme form ever attempted.

The records left by that revolutionary experiment have been widely used to discredit both the experiment itself and democratic faith in general. Yet those records need not put democracy out of countenance, nor are they wholly devoid of comfort for those of that faith. No red glow of anarchy lit up the southern horizon as a consequence of the revolution, and the enfranchised freedmen did not prove the unleashed beast of Federalist imagination. Moral pigsties undoubtedly developed, but they were oftener than not the creation of the other race, and more of them were to be found outside the South than within.

The new electorate of freedmen proved on the whole remarkably modest in their demands, unaggressive in their conduct, and deferential in their attitude. In no state did they hold place and power in anything approaching their actual numbers and voting strength. The possible exception was South Carolina, and there they held a majority of seats only in the lower house of the legislature. In the first legislature under the new constitution of Mississippi, the other state with a large Negro majority of population, Negro representatives constituted only two-sevenths of the membership of the House and an even smaller proportion of the Senate. Freedmen of that state almost never took advantage of their numbers to seize control in local government, for a Negro majority in a municipal government seems to have been unknown. There was only one Negro mayor of a city in the state and a record of only twelve sheriffs. Only three Negroes were elected in the whole country to the Forty-first Congress, the first to which they were eligible, and there were never more than eight at one time out of a total of more than one hundred members from the Southern states. In view of the subordinate role and the few offices that the freedmen took, no state in the South could properly be said to have been under Negro rule or "domination" at any time.

Yet in varying numbers and different states Negroes occupied all the varieties of public office in existence, up to but not including the governorship. They served as policemen and supreme court justices, recorders of deeds and lieutenant-governors, sheriffs and prosecuting attorneys, justices of the peace and state superintendents of education, mayors and United States senators. Without doubt some of them made awkward efforts and a few of them cut some grotesque capers, but upon the crude stage of frontier democracy comic figures had appeared before this time, and none of them could have been taken for colored minstrels before 1868. In an age of low public morals the country over, some of the neophyte politicians were as guilty of corruption as the old hands, but the neophytes rarely seem to have received their fair share of graft.

In retrospect, one is more impressed with the success that a people of such meager resources and limited experience enjoyed in producing the number of sober, honest, and capable leaders and public servants they did. The appearance of some of this sort in every state is the main comfort the record provides to the democratic faith. They give the impression of people struggling conscientiously under desperate odds to live up to a test such as no other people had ever been subjected to in all the long testing of the democratic theory. Their success varied from state to state. With regard to Mississippi the conclusions of Vernon Wharton are that "altogether, as governments go, that supplied by the Negro and white Republicans in Mississippi between 1870 and 1876 was not a bad government. Never, in states, counties, or towns, did the Negroes hold office in proportion to their numbers. . . . The Negroes who held county offices were often ignorant, but under the control of white Democrats or Republicans they supplied a form of government which differed little from that in counties where they held no offices. The three who represented the state in Congress were above reproach. Those in the legislature sought no special advantages for their race, and in one of their very first acts they petitioned Congress to remove all political disabilities from the whites. With their white Republican colleagues, they gave to the state a government of greatly expanded functions at a cost that was low in comparison with that of almost any other state."

By the operation of a sort of historical color bar, the history of the Negro's political experience in Reconstruction has been studied too much in isolation and pictured as unique. There were unique features in that history, of course, but it does not constitute the only, nor the last, instance of the sudden enfranchisement of large numbers of politically inexperienced people. Nor does it support the stereotype of the Negro as the political tyro and neophyte of the western world, the laggard in the race for political maturity. After the Reconstruction episode was over, millions of people entered this country. Of the more than twelve million white immigrants who poured into the stream of American citizenship in the fifty years after 1880 from southern and eastern European countries, it is doubtful that more than a very small percentage had ever enjoyed any significant experience of direct political participation in the democratic sense. Their first taste of such experience came in the 1880's, the 1890's, or 1900's, or later when they took out citizenship papers. Here were the real political neophytes of the American electorate. They greatly outnumber the Negro population. They too were dominated by bosses and influenced by handouts and small favors. The record of the inexperience, naïveté, and ineptitude of these erstwhile peasants in the big city slums is written in the history of corrupt city bosses, rings, and machines, a history that can match some of the darker chapters of Reconstruction government. The Mugwump reformers turned against them, as they turned against the Radical Republicans, because of the corruption associated with their regimes. Eventually the immigrants learned the ropes, gained experience and assurance, helped clean up some of the messes their inexperience had created, and gained acceptance as respected members of the body politic.

The immigrants had their own handicaps of language and prejudice to deal with, but they never had anything approaching the handicaps against which the Negro had to struggle to gain acceptance. The prejudices that the immigrants confronted were nothing like the race prejudice with which the Negro had to cope. Nor was the white immigrant's enfranchisement accompanied by the disfranchisement of the ruling and propertied classes of the community in which he settled. Neither did the exercise of his franchise have to be protected by the bayonets of federal troops, nor did the gaining of his political rights appear to old settlers as a penalty and punishment inflicted upon them, a deliberate humiliation of them by their conquerors. Political leaders of the immigrants were not ordinarily regarded by the old settlers as "carpetbaggers," intruders, and puppets of a hostile government sent to rule over them; immigrants did not regard the old settlers as their former owners, any more than the old settlers looked upon the immigrants as their former slaves. The situation of the latest political neophytes was, after all, in many ways quite different from that of the neophytes of the seventies.

The time eventually came when the incubus of their political genesis returned to haunt the freedmen and destroy their future. That was the time when the two dominant operative motives of Radical Reconstruction, party advantage and sectional business interests, became inactive—the time when it became apparent that those mighty ends could better be served by abandoning the experiment and leaving the freedmen to shift for themselves. The philanthropic motive was still a factor, and in many minds still strong, but it was not enough without the support of the two powerful props of party advantage and sectional interests. The moment of collapse came at different times in different states, but the climax and consolidation of the decision came with the disputed presidential election of 1876 and the settlement that resolved it in the Compromise of 1877.

It would be neither fair nor accurate to place all the blame upon the North and its selfish interests. There had been plenty of willing co-operation on the part of Southern whites. They had used craft and guile, force and violence, economic pressure and physical terror, and all the subtle psychological devices of race prejudice and propaganda at their command. But the Southern whites were after all a minority, and not a strong minority at that. The North had not only numbers and power on its side, but the law and the Constitution as well. When the moment of crisis arrived, however, the old doubts and skepticism of the North returned, the doubts that had kept the Negro disfranchised in the North after freedman's suffrage had been imposed upon the South. After the Fifteenth Amendment was passed, the North rapidly lost interest in the Negro voters. They were pushed out of the limelight by other interests, beset by prejudices, and neglected by politicians. The Northern Negro did not enjoy a fraction of the political success the Southern Negro enjoyed, as modest as that was. Reformers and Mugwumps of the North identified corruption with the Radical wing of the Republican party, lost interest in the Negro allies of the Radicals, and looked upon them as a means of perpetuating corrupt government all over the nation as well as in the South. In this mood they came to the conclusion that the Negro voter had been given a fair chance to prove his worth as a responsible citizen and that the experiment had proved a failure. This conclusion appeared in many places, most strangely perhaps in the columns of that old champion of the race, the New York *Tribune* (April 7, 1877), which declared that the Negroes had been given "ample opportunity to develop their own latent capacities," and had only succeeded in proving that "as a race they are idle, ignorant, and vicious."

The North's loss of faith in its own cause is reflected in many surprising places. One example must suffice. It is of special interest because it comes from the supreme official charged with enforcing the Fifteenth Amendment and guaranteeing to the freedmen their political rights, the President whose administration coincided with Radical Reconstruction and the whole great experiment—General U. S. Grant. According to the diary of Secretary Hamilton Fish, entry of January 17, 1877: "He [Grant] says he opposed the Fifteenth Amendment and thinks it was a mistake, that it had done the Negro no good, and had been

a hindrance to the South, and by no means a political advantage to the North."

During the present struggle for Negro rights, which
might be called the Second Reconstruction—though one
of quite a different sort—I have noticed among Negro in
tellectuals at times a tendency to look back upon the First
Reconstruction as if it were in some ways a sort of Golden
Age. In this nostalgic view that period takes the shape
of the race's finest hour, a time of heroic leaders and deeds,
of high faith and firm resolution, a time of forthright and
passionate action, with no bowing to compromises of
"deliberate speed." I think I understand their feeling. Reconstruction will always have a special and powerful meaning for the Negro. It is undoubtedly a period full of rich
and tragic and meaningful history, a period that should
be studiously searched for its meanings, a period that has
many meanings yet to yield. But I seriously doubt that it
will ever serve satisfactorily as a Golden Age—for anybody. There is too much irony mixed with the tragedy.

6

A Southern Critique for the Gilded Age

Melville, Adams, and James

ONE TRADITIONAL MEANS THE SOUTH EMPLOYED FOR DE-
fining its identity and keeping the image clear was the
running critique of Yankee morals it kept going over the
years. It was not invariably on the receiving end of social
criticism and moral attack. The crudities, excesses, and
shams of the Gilded Age presented Southern critics and
moralists with the broadest target they had ever had above
the Potomac. Yet this opportunity coincided ironically
with the lowest ebb of Southern influence and confidence.
A few isolated spokesmen of the old critique of Yankee
"progress" nevertheless pressed the attack with enfeebled
forces. The anonymous author of an essay entitled "The
Age of Sham" in *De Bow's Review* of 1868 typified the
scorn with which the Southern school greeted the new
industrial civilization. "Alas!" he wrote, "we have sham
idols, sham heroes, sham politicians, sham scholars, and
sham schools." The whole age was gilded with a "false

glitter, the pale mockery of the pure gold of truth, honor, and religion."

In like vein George Fitzhugh, George Frederick Holmes, Albert Taylor Bledsoe, Robert L. Dabney, and other champions of the Lost Cause continued to pronounce judgment upon the shortcomings of the new Yankee order. The combined impact of their criticism could scarcely have been more infinitesimal. Discredited from the outset, they could be readily dismissed as embittered die-hards, hopelessly outmoded, and their criticism labeled proslavery propaganda. The only Southern spokesmen who commanded national attention in that era were those of the New South school, who swelled the chorus in praise of the new order.

One of the most curious phenomena in the intellectual history of the period was that it remained for *Northern* writers, three of the most discerning critics of the age, to acknowledge the relevance of the Southern tradition and bring to bear that point of view in their critique of American society. They were Herman Melville, Henry Adams, and Henry James. Each came of an authentic Yankee heritage.

Melville employed this point of view in his long narrative and philosophical poem *Clarel* (1876), Adams in his satirical novel *Democracy* (1880), and James in his novel *The Bostonians* (1886). In each of these works a Southerner, a veteran of the Confederate Army, is introduced in a sympathetic role. His importance varies with the work concerned, but in each of the three works the Southerner serves as the mouthpiece of the severest strictures upon American society or, by his actions or character, exposes the worst faults in that society. He does not necessarily express the author's views, but the views he does express and the tradition he represents are assured a sympathetic reception.

I

In December, 1866, Herman Melville received an appointment as an outdoor inspector for the New York Customhouse. His office was on a North River wharf not far from his home, and his wages were four dollars a day. He kept the job for nineteen years. Forty-seven at the time he accepted the customhouse place, Melville was already past his literary prime and rapidly fading from public notice. In a letter written in 1872 pleading that Melville's job be spared from the spoilsmen, his brother-in-law pictured the poet in his strange environment. "Surrounded by low venality," he wrote, "he puts it all quietly aside,—quietly returning money which has been thrust into his pockets behind his back, avoiding offense alike to the corrupting merchants and their clerks and runners, who think that all men can be bought, and to the corrupt swarms who shamelessly seek their price;—quietly, steadfastly doing his duty, and happy in retaining his own self-respect." It was from this vantage point that Melville viewed the sordid postwar scene, and it was here, between 1870 and 1876, that he wrote his long poem *Clarel*.

Social criticism is only an incidental and belatedly introduced theme of the four-thousand-line poem. The major theme is the quest of the American youth Clarel for philosophical meanings. No Faustian figure, no demon-driven Ahab, Clarel is a man plagued by doubts and yearning for a tenable faith, torn between the will to believe and the impulse of skepticism. The narrative deals with a pilgrimage in the Holy Land, where Melville had traveled in 1857, and is full of problems of faith and skepticism treated earlier by Tennyson and Arnold. The argument is developed by conversations among Clarel, three other Americans, and numerous characters from other lands representing different faiths and philosophies. One of the most attractive and persuasive characters in the entourage is Derwent, an Anglican priest, a gentleman, and a thoroughly articulate Christian. Derwent found no difficulty in countering the skepticism of the less sophisticated Clarel and hedging in his arguments with doctrines of liberalism, progress, and optimism. While Clarel could not handle the arguments of his friend, he chafed impotently against what he dimly felt to be their essential complacency, even their smugness. To counter Derwent's philosophy, and one suspects to voice his own smoldering rage as well, Melville introduces the expatriate Confederate soldier Ungar.

Ungar is pictured not only as a Southern rebel but as a Southerner with Indian blood in his veins, descendant of a union between one of Calvert's cavaliers and "a wigwam maid" of Maryland. He has "an Anglo brain, but Indian heart." He is loyal to the Lost Cause, but holds slavery "a grief" and "an iniquity." He rides apart from his countrymen, taking no part at first in their discussions, and for a

long time remaining a subject of speculation and a figure
of mystery.

> His shoulders lithe
> Were long-sloped and yet ample, too,
> In keeping with each limb and thew:
> Waist flexile as a willow withe;
> Withal, a slouched reserve of strength,
> As in the pard's luxurious length;
> The cheek, high-boned, of copperish show
> Enhanced by sun on land and seas;
> Long hair, much like a Cherokee's,
> Curving behind the ear in flow
> And veiling part a sabre-scar
> Slant on the neck, a livid bar;
> Nor might the felt hat hide from view
> One temple pitted with strange blue
> Of powder-burn. Of him you'd say—
> A veteran, no more. But nay:
> Brown eyes, what reveries they keep—
> Sad woods they be, where wild things sleep. . . .
> A native of the fair South-west—
> Their countryman, though of a zone
> Varied in nature from their own:
> A countryman—but how estranged!

As a Confederate veteran and as a Southerner of Indian
heritage, Ungar is an American who has suffered two re-
jections, two defeats, and a double estrangement from his
native land. Bearing the scars of Antietam and Gettysburg,
he has fled "the immense charred solitudes" of the war-
burnt and devastated South and voluntarily entered the

service of the Turks as a mercenary soldier. In the presence of this somber and forbidding figure, optimistic talk of progress and justice turns to cant in the mouth of the kindly priest. Whether Ungar speaks as a Southerner or as part-Indian—and he speaks sometimes as one and sometimes as the other—his heritage of multiple grievances lends both motivation and authority to his bitter pronouncements upon contemporary civilization.

Ungar's first Jeremiad is prompted by the proverb, "as cruel as a Turk." He reminds Derwent that it was originated in the time of the crusades by the Anglo-Saxons, the same race that deprived the Confederacy of medicine by blockade. He continues:

> The Anglo-Saxons—lacking grace
> To win the love of any race;
> Hated by myriads dispossessed
> Of rights—the Indians East and West.
> These pirates of the sphere! grave looters—
> Grave, canting Mammonite freebooters,
> Who in the name of Christ and Trade
> (Oh, bucklered forehead of the brass!)
> Deflowered the world's last sylvan glade!

This "wandering Ishmael from the West" continued to exasperate his companions by scoffing at the idea of progress, defending the Middle Ages, and denouncing the works of capitalism. Some of them decide he is "a man of bitter blood," perverse for the sheer sake of perversity. Ungar is as harsh and unsparing in his exposure of the hypocrisies of "equality," the cruelties of "free enterprise,"

and the evils of wage slavery as ever George Fitzhugh or
John Calhoun contrived to be. Democracy is the "Arch-
strumpet of an impious age." He will concede nothing
to the optimist who cites the advance of arts and sciences
as the hope of the future:

> Your arts advance in faith's decay:
> You are but drilling the new Hun
> Whose growl even now can some dismay;
> Vindictive in his heart of hearts,
> He schools him in your mines and marts—
> A skilled destroyer.

Rolfe, one of the Americans, protests vigorously that,
while Ungar's pessimism might find justification in the
dark future of the Old World, the hope of mankind lay
in the New World. There free land and the open frontier
provided a providential safety valve to release men from
the bitter conflicts that plague the rest of the world. In
Rolfe's words:

> The vast reserves—the untried fields;
> These long shall keep off and delay
> The class-war, rich-and-poor-man fray
> Of history. From these alone
> Can serious trouble spring. Even that
> Itself, this good result may own—
> The first firm founding of the state.

Ungar would have none of this flattering unction of
nationalism. Far from an exception, America's polyglot,
materialistic society was more susceptible to the modern
forces of disintegration and brutalization than other parts

of the world. In framing the Southerner's reply to Rolfe, Herman Melville in all probability penned the blackest commentary on the future of his country ever written by an American in the nineteenth century:

> Yours seem a reasonable tone;
> But in the New World things make haste;
> Not only men, the *state* lives fast—
> Fast breeds the pregnant eggs and shells,
> The slumberous combustibles
> Sure to explode. 'Twill come, 'twill come!
> One demagogue can trouble much:
> How of a hundred thousand such?
> And universal suffrage lent
> To back them with brute element
> Overwhelming? What shall bind these seas
> Of rival sharp communities
> Unchristianized? . . .
>   Know
> Whatever happen in the end,
> Be sure 'twill yield to one and all
> New confirmation of the fall
> Of Adam. Sequel may ensue,
> Indeed, whose germs one now may view:
> Myriads playing pygmy parts—
> Debased into equality:
> In glut of all material arts
> A civic barbarism may be:
> Man disennobled—brutalized
> By popular science—atheised
> Into a smatterer . . .
>   Yet knowing all self need to know

In self's base little fallacy;
Dead level of rank commonplace:
An Anglo-Saxon China, see,
May on your vast plains shame the race
In the Dark Ages of Democracy.

2

Late one night in July, 1868, the Cunard steamer *China* sailed into New York Harbor with Henry Adams, his father and other members of the family, returning to their native land after an absence of seven years abroad. The ship anchored, and the Adamses clambered over the side into a government tugboat, which, according to Henry's account in *The Education,* "set them ashore in black darkness at the end of some North River pier."

Adams described himself as Melville, who was nearly twenty years his senior, might with more reason have done as "a survivor from the fifties." Postwar America had moved off swiftly on a new course and left him behind, "a flotsam or jetsam of wreckage," he added with a characteristic flourish of exaggeration—"a belated reveller, or a scholar-gipsy like Matthew Arnold's. His world was dead." He deemed himself no better off "than the Indians or the buffalo who had been ejected from their heritage by his own people."

Within three months after his return Adams had moved to Washington and made a successful start in a career of journalism. His specialty was exposure, and as the Grant administration developed, the rich variety of things to be exposed multiplied too fast to permit any journalist to keep pace. The young writer moved from one scandal to the next, seeking to learn whether there were any limit to the depth of degradation into which American democracy was sinking. He was sure that "Grant's administration outraged every rule of ordinary decency," and he later concluded that "one might search the whole list of Congress, Judiciary, and Executive during the twenty-five years 1870 to 1895, and find little but damaged reputation."

Disgusted with the scene after two years, Adams withdrew to teach history at Harvard from 1870 to 1877. In the latter year, however, after marrying and resigning his position, he returned to Washington. There he established his home on Lafayette Square opposite the White House, resumed his role as spectator, and continued his ruminations about the fate of democracy. His main intellectual activity in the years that followed was devoted to writing his big history of the Jefferson and Madison administrations. Although he had given up journalism, he had never lost the journalist's absorption in the current scene and his urge to express himself on the subject. In the mature Adams this urge found expression in the novel *Democracy,* which he published anonymously in 1880.

The protagonist of the novel is Mrs. Lightfoot Lee, a wealthy and sophisticated native of Philadelphia, thirty years of age and quite attractive. She had lost her husband, a descendant of one branch of the Virginia Lees who had drifted to New York, and her only child. The ordeal of tragedy had left her, so she thought, "pure steel." Mrs. Lee had read "voraciously and promiscuously" but had found solace neither in German philosophy nor in the amusements of the international set in which she moved. In her restlessness and discontent she decides to move to Washington to explore the secrets of power. As Adams describes her motives, "She wanted to see with her own eyes the action of primary forces; to touch with her own hand the massive machinery of society; to measure with her own mind the capacity of the motive power. She was bent upon getting to the heart of the great American mystery of democracy and government." The author hints that her curiosity was not wholly disinterested. "What she wanted," he adds, "was Power."

Mrs. Lee moved to Washington with her sister Sybil Ross and rented a house on Lafayette Square in what would seem to have been December, 1876, about the time the Henry Adamses took the same step. What follows, according to Adams' biographer Ernest Samuels, "is little more than veiled autobiography, the life and opinions of Henry Adams and his Washington circle in 1878–79." Madeleine Lee, who bore some resemblance to Marian Adams, quickly attracted an exclusive salon made up of kindred spirits and a few specimens of a different sort carefully selected for close study.

Among the latter type admitted to her salon is Senator Silas P. Ratcliffe of Illinois, dictator of his party and ambitious to become President. He had recently missed the nomination by three votes, and he was at the moment engaged in bringing the President-elect completely under his power. He combined some of the traits of Senator James G. Blaine with some of the characteristics of Senator Roscoe Conkling. The press stood in awe of "the Prairie Giant from Peonia," and so did other powerful forces of society. Senator Ratcliffe presents Madeleine Lee with an opportunity for satisfying not only her curiosity but her ambition. For the Senator not only stands very close to "the great American mystery of democracy and government" that Mrs. Lee is trying to solve, but he is also looking for a wife.

For all the mastery and power he attributes to Ratcliffe, Adams paints a highly unattractive picture of the Senator. Fifty years of age, he is at the peak of his political power and prestige. Born and educated in New England, he moved West and "fresh from that hot-bed of abolition, . . . threw himself into the anti-slavery movement in Illinois," where "after a long struggle he rose with the wave." He is "a handsome man and still in his prime," but there is "a certain coarse and animal expression about the mouth, and an indefinable coldness in the eye." * An avowed cynic about reform and morality in politics, Ratcliffe undertakes to persuade Madeleine Lee of the essential correctness and inevitability of his Machiavellian code.

* In his essay "The Great Secession Winter of 1860–61," written in 1861, Adams described Senator Stephen A. Douglas of Illinois as a "coarse politician" with "animal features." The extent of the historian's involvement in partisan rivalries and the effect upon his judgment are suggested by his further statement that "no man in the whole nation has done so much as he [Douglas] to degrade the standard of political morality and to further the efforts of the slave power."

All that stands in the way of Ratcliffe's conquest of the mind and heart of Mrs. Lee as it turns out in the end is John Carrington, Virginian. In marked contrast with the portrait of Ratcliffe, Adams' picture of Carrington is colored with great warmth and sympathy. A distant kinsman of her husband, Carrington was accepted as friend and mentor by Madeleine Lee from the start, because he was "a man whom she liked, and because he was one whom life had treated hardly." He was "of that unfortunate generation in the south which began existence with civil war," and he had fought four years in the Confederate Army. Madeleine's sister Sybil sees him as a man who "had grown used to the shocks of fate, so as to walk with calmness into the face of death, and to command or obey with equal indifference." And Madeleine herself, who "trusted in him by instinct," declared that "he is my idea of George Washington at thirty." The association of Carrington with Washington is deliberate, and to emphasize the point the novelist has another lady refer to him later, only half in jest, as "General Washington restored to us in his prime."

A lagging law practice leaves Carrington plenty of time to serve Mrs. Lee, of whom he soon becomes secretly enamored, as guide through national politics. Ratcliffe is ready with his suggestions as well. The charming explorer of the Washington jungle concludes that she needs all the help she can get when she contemplates "this maze of personal intrigue, this wilderness of stunted natures where no straight road was to be found, but only the tortuous and aimless tracks of beasts and things that crawl." Both the horror and the fascination of the spectacle grow upon her as she learns more of "the illiterate swarm" of congressmen, watches "the dance of democracy round the president," tests "the quagmire of politics," and attempts to sound the depths of "this ocean of corruption."

Across the Potomac, in striking contrast to the city built in swamps and sunk in quagmires of corruption, rise the stately white Virginia mansions of Arlington and Mount Vernon. They constitute a grave and silent censure of the scene below, and it is to these vantage points on the Virginia bank of the river that the novelist has his characters repair for their deeper colloquies on the future of democracy. On a picnic at Mount Vernon, Mrs. Lee sighs over the peace and dignity of the old place and exclaims, "And yet that dreadful Capitol and its office-seekers are only ten miles off." A flippant debutante tries a bit of modern irreverence at the expense of the old hero, but Nathan Gore, the only New Englander present, breaks into an impassioned tribute. He admits that Washington cared little for New England but declares that "for all that, we idolize him. To us he is Morality, Justice, Duty, Truth; half a dozen Roman gods with capital letters. He is austere, solitary, grand; he ought to be deified." Carrington, whose family "had been deep in the confidence of Washington himself," proves reticent in his comments and prefers to draw out the opinions of Senator Ratcliffe. The Senator obliges with some reflections of which Madeleine Lee takes careful note. "If Washington were President now," he observes, "he would have to learn our ways or lose his next election. . . . If virtue won't answer our purposes, we must use vice, or our opponents will put us out of office, and this was as true in Washington's day as it is now, and always will be."

Later the scene is the portico of the home of General Robert E. Lee at Arlington, where Carrington and Madeleine's sister sit one day after a pensive ride. "From the heavy brick porch they looked across the superb river to the raw and incoherent ugliness of the city." Carrington says that he would rather not go into the house, long ago gutted by looters. He explains that the Lees were old family friends and that he has memories of many happy days as a guest in the old home. Sybil is startled by "the long white ranks of head-stones, stretching up and down the hill-sides by thousands, in order of battle," and is shocked at the thought that her handsome and silent companion had borne arms against these men who had fought for her cause. In spite of this she reflects that "he gained dignity in his rebel isolation." Once again the novelist deliberately associates valor, honor, dignity, and the heroic traditions of the past—of whichever side—with Virginia soil and name and place.

In the meantime the widow continues her pursuit of "the great American mystery" and in doing so falls deeper under the powerful influence of Ratcliffe. The Senator flatters her vanity by disclosing deep secrets of state, revealing foibles of the mighty, confronting her with the moral dilemmas of the weighty decisions he is forced to make, and insisting that she apply her fine ideals to these problems, tell him what to do, and thus share the responsibility and the guilt of such compromises as he seeks to justify in her eyes. "She reconciled herself to accepting the Ratcliffian morals," we are told, "for she could see no choice. She herself had approved every step she had seen him take. She could not deny that there must be something wrong in a double standard of morality, but where was it? Mr. Ratcliffe seemed to her to be doing good work with as pure means as he had at hand. He ought to be encouraged, not reviled. What was she that she should stand in judgment?"

Another argument is silently but eloquently pressed against the widow's defenses. If she is really serious about her desire to improve and reform American politics or, for that matter, in earnest about penetrating its mysteries, what better opportunity could she ask than that of becoming the wife of the most powerful politician in the country? She has had no lack of opportunities to witness the commanding power and crushing influence he wields. She has sat in the gallery and watched him sway the Senate with his eloquence, and she has seen a new President of the United States knuckle under to his influence. Madeleine Lee's resistance gradually crumbles under the assault of Ratcliffe's tactics and her own ambition for power.

John Carrington watches in horror but in relative helplessness. He regards Ratcliffe as the very "spirit of evil," a moral monster, and he has definite proof that the politician has recently sold his influence for a huge bribe. But he is restrained from using his knowledge against the corrupt Senator by two considerations. For one thing, professional ethics keep him from disclosing the evidence of Ratcliffe's guilt, since it came into his hands through the confidence of a client. For another, his own suit has been gently rejected by Mrs. Lee, and she has already flared up resentfully at his attempts to warn her against the danger she is in.

Ratcliffe has arranged the climax of his campaign to perfection. Carrington has been unwittingly maneuvered out of the scene by accepting a mission to Mexico, which the Senator has secretly arranged. Madeleine has been escorted to the peaks of social and political prestige at a colossal ball for European royalty, and at this advantageous moment Ratcliffe makes his proposal. He puts his case so forcefully and persuasively that Mrs. Lee is about won over. She promises him her answer the next day. Then in the nick of time sister Sybil springs the letter Carrington has prepared as a final resort, revealing the story of the Senator selling out to the notorious Ship Subsidy Lobby for $100,000.

Still undaunted when he is confronted with this letter, Ratcliffe defends his action with the familiar ethic of higher necessity he has advanced repeatedly. The money was necessary to buy an election that was "almost as important to the nation as the result of the war itself," since the purchased election kept the government from falling "into the blood-stained hands of rebels."

Mrs. Lee listens, fascinated, convinced that at last she has really "got to the heart of politics, so that she could, like a physician with his stethoscope, measure the organic disease." Then she realizes that her suitor "talked about virtue and vice as a man who is colour-blind talks about red and green." Here she is "face to face with a moral lunatic" who is proposing marriage so that "she could go out to the shore of this ocean of corruption, and repeat the ancient *rôle* of King Canute, or Dame Partington with her mop and pail. What was to be done with such an animal?" She settles the problem by sending the Senator packing in a blind, frustrated rage and by fleeing to Europe herself. The fable concludes with a romantic hint that the Virginia hero will yet be successful in his suit for the hand of the fair lady whom he has released from the spell of the wicked corruptionist.

3

A great part of the sport of publishing *Democracy* anonymously and keeping the secret so well lay in the fun that Henry and Marian Adams got out of listening to their friends innocently speculate about its authorship and pass uninhibited judgment on the novel's merits, or lack of them. The wife of the English historian John Richard Green, for example, wrote Mrs. Adams: "I hope you enjoyed *Democracy* as much as we did. Mr. [Henry] James looked very severe and grave over it, but I am not sure whether it was on patriotic or artistic grounds."

Neither James nor the Greens, though old friends of the Adamses, were in on the secret of the novel's authorship. There can be little doubt, however, that if Henry James really did pull a long face over *Democracy* it was not on "patriotic grounds." The expatriate novelist could hold his own with the Adamses in caustic criticism and patronizing comment on the shortcomings of American culture. In fact, when James and the Adamses gathered, either in London or Washington, Henry and Marian Adams found themselves invariably cast in the role of patriots defending their outraged fellow countrymen from James' attacks. During the novelist's visit with the Adamses at Washington in January, 1882, Adams remarked of James' fastidious disdain for the national capital that "poor Henry James thinks it revolting in respect to politics and the intrigues that surround it."

James himself was soon contemplating a novel of social criticism on America. He was at the first peak of his creative power in the eighties, determined, he said, to "do something great," and to "prove that I *can* write an American novel." With regard to the novel he did publish in 1886, he wrote: "I wished to write a very *American* tale, a tale very characteristic of our social conditions, and I asked myself what was the most salient and peculiar point in our social life. The answer was: the situation of women, the decline of the sentiment of sex, the agitation in their behalf." Once he got started on the novel in 1884 he wrote enthusiastically to his brother William: "It is a better subject than I have ever had before, and I think will be much the best thing I have done yet. It is called *The Bostonians*. I shall be much abused for the title, but it exactly and literally fits the story, and is much the best, simplest and most dignified I could have chosen."

Like Adams' *Democracy*, James' *Bostonians* had as a central figure a woman with a will to power, but there the resemblance between the two characters stopped. There could, in fact, scarcely be any sharper contrast in fiction than that between the vibrant, charming, outgoing personality of Madeleine Lee and the introverted, neurotic, and furtive personality of Olive Chancellor, the Boston reformer and champion of woman's rights. James' portrait of her is unrelieved in its harshness and totally unsympathetic in its severity. Her eyes were not merely described as green but recalled "the glitter of green ice." Her smile was not simply wan and cold but suggested "a thin ray of moonlight resting upon the wall of a prison." She had "pointed features and nervous manner" and "it was as plain as day that she was morbid." In fact, she "was subject to fits of tragic shyness, during which she was unable to meet even her own eyes in the mirror." Her fondest ambition was that "she might be a martyr and die for something." To complete the picture of this unfortunate young woman, "she had absolutely no figure," and "she was a woman without laughter." Her very existence was a denial of femininity and sex. To make the point explicit, James writes: "There are women who are unmarried by accident, and others who are unmarried by option; but Olive Chancellor was unmarried by every implication of her being. She was a spinster as Shelley was a lyric poet, or as the month of August is sultry." The figure amounted virtually to a caricature of the Boston bluestocking, radical, and reformer.

More important is Basil Ransom, Southerner, protagonist of the novel and the very antithesis of everything Olive Chancellor represents. He is described in heroic terms as "tall and lean, dressed throughout in black," a sort of Confederate Hamlet with a "superior head" fit for "a bronze medal," a forehead that is "high and broad, and his thick black hair, perfectly straight and glossy," is worn in "a leonine manner." He has "magnificent eyes" that are "dark, deep, and glowing," full of "smouldering fire." These characteristics, says James, "might have indicated that he was to be a great American statesman; or, on the other hand, they might simply have proved that he came from Carolina or Alabama." He came in fact from Mississippi, the cultural antipodes of Massachusetts, and spoke in an accent "pervaded by something sultry and vast, something almost African in its rich basking tone, something that suggested the teeming expanse of the cotton field," but in which there was "nothing vulgar or vain." Not one to take pleasantries about his provincial origins lightly, he replied to the chafing of a flirtatious widow, "When I dine out I usually carry a six-shooter and a bowie knife."

The son of a wealthy planter, Ransom had "tasted all the cruelty of defeat." He returned from the war to find family, property, and home ruined. After a futile attempt to make a go of the plantation, he gave up his patrimony to mother and sisters and headed for New York to practice law, "with fifty dollars in his pocket and a gnawing hunger in his heart." This was in the seventies, and he was not quite thirty years old.

In what appears to have been an uncharacteristic impulse, Olive Chancellor, who was a remote cousin and a bit younger than Ransom, invited him to visit her in Boston. Antipathy pops and crackles the length of her Back Bay drawing room at the first contact between Bluestocking and Mississippian. "Don't you care for human progress?" asks Miss Chancellor. The answer comes in a carefully courteous drawl: "I don't know—I never saw any." These are the opening guns of a duel that continues intermittently throughout the book. Ransom is well armed for the encounter. He is described as "a young man of first-rate intelligence" who "had read everything." His favorite moderns were de Tocqueville and Carlyle, but he had read his Comte as well and had no difficulty holding up his end of the argument.

Cultural contrasts are multiplied and cousinly amity further deteriorates at a meeting of Boston reformers consisting of woman's-rights people, mesmerists, spiritualists, utopians, and faded abolitionists. Ransom is all ears and repressed hilarity at his opportunity to observe these specimens in their native habitat. The gaunt hall designed for plain living and high thinking is presided over by Miss Birdseye, whom Miss Chancellor admires as "one of the earliest, one of the most passionate, of the old Abolitionists," and whom James describes as "a confused, entangled, inconsequent, discursive old woman, whose charity began at home and ended nowhere, whose credulity kept pace with it, and who knew less about her fellow-creatures, if possible, after fifty years of humanitary zeal, than on the day she had gone into the field to testify against the iniquity of most arrangements." *

The outstanding feature of the evening was an unrehearsed performance by a very pretty young woman named

---

* The author was intensely embarrassed when Elizabeth Peabody, Hawthorne's sister-in-law, was taken to be the original of Miss Birdseye.

Verena Tarrant, who had a strange gift for "inspirational" speaking. Her father, a mesmeric healer, was the prototype of "the detested carpetbagger . . . false, cunning, vulgar, ignoble; the cheapest kind of human product," and her mother, the daughter of the most famous of the Boston abolitionists. "Want to try a little inspiration?" her father would ask and, by laying on of pallid hands, would induce one of Verena's trances. Fascinated by the girl and captivated by her performance, Olive Chancellor determines immediately to rescue Verena from her impossible parents, take the girl into her own home, and see that her queer talent and her whole life are dedicated to promoting a strange brand of feminism. Verena moves in with Olive, and there begins what James calls "one of those friendships between women which are so common in New England." Olive's proposal was: "Will you be my friend, my friend of friends, beyond every one, everything, forever and forever?" One of their embraces is interrupted by an intruder who remarks, "You ladies better look out, or you'll freeze together."

Basil Ransom is equally captivated by Verena but plans a very different future for her. He is convinced that she is "made for love," his own kind of traditional, domestic, male-dominated, familial love, and that he must rescue her from the perverse sexuality of his cousin and from the quackery of the woman's-rights lecture platform. There ensues a struggle between the Mississippian and the Bostonian for the future of Verena which is comparable to the struggle between the Virginian and the Midwesterner over Madeleine Lee, except that Verena is a more passive participant and the strange courtship is carried on in socio-logical rather than in political terms.

Ransom's defense of marriage, family, tradition, and chivalry is a merciless onslaught upon the cant of the age, the cant about progress, equality, universal education, and the emancipation of women. Verena has never in her life heard such irreverence about the values she has been taught to cherish, such shocking cynicism from a professed conservative. She has "never encountered such a power of disparagement or heard so much sarcasm leveled at the institutions of her country and the tendencies of the age." And all this in such mellow, exotic, and seductive cadences, that it was all the harder to resist. "She thought conserva-tives were only smug and stubborn and self-complacent, satisfied with what actually existed; but Mr. Ransom didn't seem any more satisfied with what existed than with what she wanted to exist, and he was ready to say worse things about some of those whom she would have supposed to be on his own side than she thought it right to say about almost anyone."

It was little wonder that in her effort to keep her influ-ence over Verena, not to mention her self-respect, Olive Chancellor "made up her mind that there was no menace so great as the menace of Basil Ransom." She lectured the wavering Verena upon "male grossness" and reminded her of the pathos of "the bullied wives, the stricken mothers, the dishonored, deserted maidens," all the woes of woman-hood at male hands. "I'll tell you what is the matter with you," she says to Verena, "—you don't dislike men as a

class." Verena admitted as much and finally agreed to
be spirited away beyond the reach of Ransom while she
rehearses for the great event Olive had prepared, her debut
as a woman's-rights wonder-worker before a vast audience of Bostonians.

In the final scene, all Boston waits for Verena in the
Music Hall with growing impatience. When she does not
appear, the audience bursts out in hisses and catcalls for
Olive Chancellor. Backstage, in the meantime, the ardent
Mississippian finally persuades Verena to throw over Olive,
woman's rights, mesmerism, Boston, and the impatient
Music Hall audience and flee it all with him. He whisks
her away from the mob somewhat unromantically in a
horse car.

The last touch of irony is not the only one by which
James acknowledges that his young hero does not always
stay safely this side of the preposterous. But before concluding, the novelist puts one speech in the mouth of Ransom that, for rhetorical savagery, rivals Clarel's lines on
the Dark Ages of Democracy. "Mr. Ransom," declares
Verena angrily, "I assure you this is an age of conscience."
And he replies, "That's a part of your cant. It's an age of
unspeakable shams." The trouble lies in "feminization"
or in the decline of sexuality:

"The whole generation is womanized; the masculine
tone is passing out of the world; it's a feminine, a nervous, hysterical, chattering, canting age, an age of hollow
phrases and false delicacy and exaggerated solicitudes and
coddled sensibilities, which, if we don't soon look out, will

usher in the reign of mediocrity, of the feeblest and flattest and the most pretentious that has ever been."

4

How is one to account for the selection of a Confederate censor for Yankee morals by three of the North's most gifted literary figures and perceptive critics? Certainly the answer is not to be found in any discoverable Southern leanings or connections among them during or before the Civil War. So far as the records reveal, all came of Yankee forebears and, in the cases of Adams and Melville, a long line of them. Although none of the three writers served the Union cause in a military way, all were thoroughly loyal to that cause. Adams served it ably on the diplomatic front and Melville in his war poems. James' writing career did not start until after the war, but he was a loyal patriot. None of them could claim any personal familiarity with the South or a circle of Southern acquaintances that amounted to anything. With the exception of Melville, who lectured as far south as Tennessee in the mid-fifties, visited the Wilderness battle line, and paid his respects to Grant at Culpeper, Virginia, in 1864, none of the three had done more than set foot on Southern soil.

Yet from very early in his life the South evoked ambivalent attitudes in Henry Adams. On his first contact with a slave society at the age of twelve, when his father took him to visit Washington in 1850, he felt both repulsion and attraction. His first response was that of a true grand-

son of John Quincy Adams. "Slave States were dirty, un-
kempt, poverty-stricken, ignorant, vicious! He had not a
thought but repulsion for it [slavery]; and yet the picture
had another side." The other side, he speculated, might
have been "his Johnson blood," that of his grandmother,
who though born in England came of Maryland stock.
"The May sunshine and shadow had something to do
with it; the thickness of foliage and the heavy smells had
more; the sense of atmosphere, almost new, had perhaps
as much again; and the brooding indolence of a warm
climate and a negro population hung in the atmosphere
heavier than the catalpas. The impression was not simple, but the boy liked it: distinctly it remained on his
mind as an attraction, almost obscuring Quincy itself."
Memory of the trip left another long-lasting impression,
that of a carriage trip with his father over a very bad
road to visit Mount Vernon. "Bad roads meant bad morals"
to the New England mind. "The moral of this Virginia
road was clear, and the boy fully learned it. Slavery was
wicked, and slavery was the cause of this road's badness
which amounted to a social crime—and yet, at the end
of the road and product of the crime stood Mount Vernon
and George Washington."

Henry Adams had not ceased pondering the apparent
paradox of Southern wickedness producing George Washington when, more than a half century later, he was writing his *Education*. "George Washington could not be
reached on Boston lines," he reflected. "George Washington was a primary, or, if Virginians liked it better, an
ultimate relation, like the Pole Star, and amid the endless

restless motion of every other visible point in space, he alone remained steady, in the mind of Henry Adams, to the end." It was a pity, he reflected, that he had never thought to ask his father "how to deal with the moral problem that deduced George Washington from the sum of all wickedness." Clearly the problem was still on his mind while he was writing *Democracy,* but he was under no illusion that the novel had solved it.

The ambivalence of Henry Adams' attitude toward the South was matched by a similar complexity in the approach of Henry James toward Southerners and their section. James knew even fewer Southerners and less about the South than Adams or Melville. In fact he never crossed the Potomac until after his career as a novelist was finished, and his acquaintances among people of the region were casual and few in number. In a letter to William James about the weaknesses of *The Bostonians,* he complains of "the sense of knowing terribly little about the kind of life I had attempted to describe." He may have been referring in part to Boston, but after all he had lived in that city, and he had not so much as visited the South.

In his autobiographical work, *A Small Boy and Others,* James tells of the deep impression left on him as a child of ten by a family of Kentuckians named Norcom, who moved into the James' block on Washington Square in 1853. The child's imagination was stirred by "the southern glow of the Norcoms" which seemed to light up the whole community. In particular he was impressed by "the large, the lavish, ease of their hospitality," which took (for a ten-year-old) the gratifying form of free-handed dispensing of sausages, johnny-cakes, and molasses. "They didn't count and didn't grudge—the sausage-mill kept turning and the molasses flowing for all who came." From the safely neutral ground of New York he was already contrasting the Southern temperament with the New England character. "We were provided by their [Norcoms'] presence," he recalled, "with as happy a foil as we could have wished to the plainness and dryness of the Wards," another family of friends whom he described as "all New England." Professor Charles R. Anderson has pointed out a marked similarity between James' description of young Eugene Norcom who, he said, "haunted my imagination," and his description of Basil Ransom. As a matter of fact, James confesses naïvely how "absurdly and disproportionately" the childhood acquaintance with the Norcoms "had helped one to 'know Southerners.'"

It is doubtful that any one of the three writers, Melville least of all, was very seriously concerned to "know Southerners" or to bother themselves very deeply about the problem of Southern identity and heritage. What they *were* all deeply concerned about was what had overtaken their own society since the Civil War, the mediocrity, the crassness, and the venality they saw around them. The South or the Southern hero, past or present, was a useful foil for the unlovely present or the symbol of some irreparable loss. "Why do I feel unclean when I look at Mount Vernon?" asks Madeleine Lee.

Loyal Northerners all, Melville, Adams, and James are not always able to use their Southern viewpoint with entire confidence or without some manifestations of embarrassment and guilt. Each takes pains to have his hero disavow slavery, and Ransom and Carrington are made to abandon the principle of secession as well. Thus purged of the more troublesome doctrinal heresies, the ex-rebels prove less of an embarrassment in polite Northern company. Adams makes Carrington a unionist who fought unenthusiastically for the Confederacy; James carries the device of dissociation to the point of equivocation by referring in his own voice to the "false pride" and "moral tinsel" of the very tradition he presents to his reader as the standpoint from which to judge the Bostonians.

Common to the three writers was a tacit assumption that the war really was a civil war. Its significance was not confined to the abolition of slavery as an afterthought. America's triumph over the South did not mean simply the defeat of an external foe that left the victorious power unchanged and inflicted change and revolution upon the vanquished alone. It also meant the defeat or denial of something within, a tradition perhaps once shared with the fallen rebels, something that shared the downfall of the South. In their search for what was missing in postwar America, these Northern writers turned southward and invoked a tradition only lately renounced.

Each of them was in some degree estranged from the new America and rejected its dominant values. Each in some fashion withdrew, Melville to the obscurity of the customhouse, James to Europe as an expatriate, and Adams to the retreat of a cynical spectator. In spite of the disparity in their ages, each tended to identify himself with the past, with some older period or tradition. Adams called himself "a survivor from the fifties" whose "world was dead." James preferred the Old World and could stand the new America only in small doses. Melville could not stand much of it at any time, and it could not have cared less for him or his art.

When they came to frame their critique of the new order, they turned to the South in search of the values and traditions they had lost. Something of what they sought was really there or had been, and some of it they merely imagined. As Professor Anderson has observed, Henry James constructed a fable of Carolina as an Old World survival to which he clung to the end, and at an advanced age he sought corroboration of his fable in a tour. In the quiet old mansions of Charleston he discovered "the fallen pride of provincial palazzini," in the walled gardens he was reminded of a "little old-world quarter of quiet convents" and of the fine sense of privacy they symbolized, "One sacrificed the North on the spot." In the sea islands he imagined the "possible site of some Venice that had never mustered." He admitted the absurdity of expecting "Charleston and Savannah to betray the moral accent of Naples or Seville," but he continued his quest nevertheless.

Henry Adams was in quest of no European antiquities when he turned South, but he definitely was in search of American antiquities, the antique valor and probity of the early Republic. As a child of twelve he had decided that "Mount Vernon was only Quincy in a Southern setting. No doubt it was much more charming, but it was the same eighteenth century, the same old furniture, the same old patriot, and the same old President." Later on he was not so certain of the identity of Mount Vernon and Quincy. When Madeleine Lee asks John Carrington if he regrets the passing of the old order for which he fought, he replies: "One can't help regretting whatever it was that produced George Washington, and a crowd of other men like him." The problem of Mount Vernon and "the sum of all wickedness" was still gnawing at the mind of Henry Adams.

Among the ghosts of the Old Regime that haunted the deep woods across the Potomac there must have been a good deal of wry merriment from time to time over the modern turn of events. The taste for irony could hardly have been better served, in fact, than by the belated Yankee deference implicit in the selection of Confederate censors for Yankee morals.

7

The Populist Heritage and the Intellectual

THIRTY YEARS AFTER SECESSION AND CIVIL WAR, THE South suffered a second alienation from the dominant national spirit. This received expression in the Populist upheaval of the nineties. The Populist movement won more sympathy in the West than had the Secessionist movement. It did not win the allegiance of as large a proportion of Southerners as had the Lost Cause, nor did it involve those it did win quite so deeply. But the alienation was real enough, and the heritage it left was a lasting one.

During the long era of the New Deal, one had little difficulty living in comparative congeniality with the Populist heritage. The two periods had much in common, and it was easy to exaggerate the similarities and natural to seek antecedents and analogies in the earlier era. Because of the common setting of severe depression and economic dislocation, Populism seemed even closer to the New Deal than did Progressivism, which had a setting of prosperity. Common to both Populists and New Dealers was an antagonism to the values and dominant leaders of the business community. Among both was a sense of urgency and an edge of desperation about the demand for reform. And in both, so far as the South and West were concerned, agricultural problems were the most desperate, and agrarian reforms occupied the center of attention. It seemed entirely fitting that Hugo Black of Alabama and Harry Truman of Missouri—politicians whose political style and heritage were strongly Populistic—should lead New Deal reform battles. From many points of view the New Deal was neo-Populism.

The neo-Populism of the present bred a Populistic view of the past. American historiography of the 1930's and 1940's reflects a strong persuasion of this sort. The most popular college textbook in American history was written by a Midwesterner, John D. Hicks, who was friendly to Populism and the foremost historian of the movement. The leading competitor of this book was one that shared many of the Populist leanings, even though one of its authors was a Harvard patrician and the other a Columbia urbanite. A remarkably heterogeneous assortment of men and ideas struck up congenial ties in the neo-Populist coalition. Small-town Southerners and big-city Northerners, Texas mavericks and Hudson River aristocrats, Chapel Hill liberals and Nashville agrarians were all able to discover some sort of identity in the heritage. The South rediscovered ties with the West, the farmer with labor. The New York-Virginia axis was revived. Jacksonians were found to have urban affiliations and origins. Not to be outdone, the Communists staked out claim to selected Populist heroes.

Many intellectuals made themselves at home in the neo-Populist coalition and embraced the Populist heritage. They had prepared the way for the affiliation in the twenties when they broke with the genteel tradition, adopted the mucker pose, and decided that conventional politics and the two major parties were the province of the boobocracy and professional politicians were clowns or hypocrites. In the thirties intellectuals made naïve identification with farmers and workers and supported their spokesmen with enthusiasm. The Populist affinity outlasted the New Deal, survived the war, and perhaps found its fullest expression in the spirit of indulgent affection with which intellectuals often supported Harry Truman and his administration.

Even before Truman left the White House, however, the Populist identification fell into disgrace, and intellectuals began to repudiate the heritage. "Populist" suddenly became a term of opprobrium, in some circles a pejorative epithet. This resulted from no transfer of affection to Truman's successor, for there was very little of that among intellectuals. The origins of the altered temper came earlier.

Disenchantment of the intellectual with the masses was well under way in the forties. Mass support for evil causes in Germany and elsewhere helped to undermine the faith. The liberal's feelings of guilt and impotence were reflected in the interest that the writings of Sören Kierkegaard and Reinhold Niebuhr aroused, and the mood of self-flagellation was expressed in the vogue of the novels of Franz Kafka and George Orwell. The shock of the encounter with McCarthyism sustained and intensified the mood. Liberals and intellectuals bore the brunt of the Mc-Carthyite assault on standards of decency. They were rightly alarmed and felt themselves betrayed. They were the victims of a perversion of the democracy they cherished, a seamy and sinister side of democracy to which they now guiltily realized they had too often turned a blind or indulgent eye. Stung by consciousness of their own naïveté, they responded with a healthy impulse to make up for lost time and confront their problem with all the critical resources at their command. The consequence has been a formidable and often valuable corpus of social criticism.

Not one of the critics, not even the most conservative, is prepared to repudiate democracy. There is general agreement that the fault lay in some abuse or perversion of democracy and was not inherent in democracy itself. All the critics are aware that these abuses and perversions had historic antecedents and had appeared in various guises and with disturbing frequency in national history. These unhappy tendencies were varously described as "mobbism," "direct democracy," or "plebiscitarianism," but there is a surprising and apparently spontaneous consensus of preference for "Populism." Although the word is usually capitalized, the critics do not as a rule limit its reference to the political party that gave currency to the term. While there is general agreement that the essential characteristics designated by the term are best illustrated by an agrarian movement in the last decade of the nineteenth century, some of the critics take the liberty of applying it to movements as early as the Jacksonians, or earlier, and to twentieth-century phenomena as well.

Reasons for this convergence from several angles upon "Populism" as the appropriate designation for an abhorred abuse are not all clear. A few, however, suggest themselves. Populism is popularly thought of as an entirely Western affair, Wisconsin as a seedbed of the movement, and Old Bob La Follette as a foremost exponent. None of these assumptions is historically warranted, but it is true that Senator McCarthy came from Wisconsin, that much of his support came from the Middle West, and that there are some similarities between the two movements. The impression of similarity has been enhanced by the historical echo of their own alarm that modern intellectuals have caught in the rather hysterical fright with which Eastern conservatives reacted to Populism in the nineties.

This essay is not concerned with the validity of recent analysis of the "radical right" and its fascistic manifestations in America. It is concerned only with the tendency to identify Populism with these movements and with the implied rejection of the Populist tradition. It is admittedly very difficult, without risk of misrepresentation and injustice, to generalize about the way in which numerous critics have employed the Populist identification. They differ widely in the meaning they attribute to the term and the importance they attach to the identification. Among the critics are sociologists, political scientists, poets, and journalists, as well as historians, and there is naturally a diversity in the degree of historical awareness and competence they command. Among points of view represented are the New Conservative, the New Liberal, the liberal progressive, the Jewish, the Anglophile, and the urban, with some overlapping. There is no conscious spokesmen of the West or the South, but some are more or less unconscious representatives of the urban East. Every effort will be made not to attribute to one the views of another.*

Certain concessions are due on the outset. Any fairminded historian will acknowledge the validity of some of the points scored by the new critics against the Populist tradition and its defenses. It is undoubtedly true that liberal intellectuals have in the past constructed a flattering image of Populism. They have permitted their sympathy with oppressed groups to blind them to the delusions, myths, and foibles of the people with whom they sympathized. Sharing certain political and economic doctrines and certain indignations with the Populists, they have attributed to them other values, tastes, principles, and morals which the Populists did not actually share. It was understandably distasteful to dwell upon the irrational or retrograde traits of people who deserved one's sympathy and

---

* Daniel Bell (ed.), *The New American Right* (New York, 1955), especially essays by Richard Hofstadter, Peter Viereck, Talcott Parsons, and Seymour Martin Lipset; Edward A. Shils, *The Torment of Secrecy* (Glencoe, Ill., 1956) and "The Intellectuals and the Powers: Some Perspectives for Comparative Analysis" in *Comparative Studies in Society and History,* I (October, 1958), 5–22; Peter Viereck, *The Unadjusted Man* (Boston, 1956); Oscar Handlin, *Race and Nationality in American Life* (Boston, 1957), and "American Views of the Jews at the Opening of the Twentieth Century," *Publication of the American Jewish Historical Society,* No. 40 (June, 1951), 323–44; Richard Hofstadter, *The Age of Reform* (New York, 1955); Victor C. Ferkiss, "Ezra Pound and American Fascism," *Journal of Politics,* XVII (1955), 174–96; Max Lerner, *America as a Civilization* (New York, 1958).

shared some of one's views. For undertaking this neglected and distasteful task in the spirit of civility and forbearance which, for example, Richard Hofstadter has shown, some of the new critics deserve much credit. All of them concede some measure of value in the Populist heritage, though none so handsomely as Hofstadter, who assumes that Populism and Progressivism are strongly enough established in our tradition to withstand criticism. Others are prone to make their concessions more perfunctory and to hasten on with the job of heaping upon Populism, as upon an historical scapegoat, all the ills to which democracy is heir.

The danger is that under the concentrated impact of the new criticism the risk is incurred, not only of blurring a historical image, but of swapping an old stereotype for a new one. The old one sometimes approached the formulation that Populism is the root of all good in democracy, while the new one sometimes suggests that Populism is the root of all evil. Uncritical repetition and occasional exaggeration of the strictures of some of the critics threaten to result in establishing a new maxim in American political thought: *Radix malorum est Populismus.*

Few of the critics engaged in the reassessment of Populism and the analysis of the New American Right would perhaps go quite so far as Peter Viereck, when he writes that "beneath the sane economic demands of the Populists of 1880–1900 seethed a mania of xenophobia, Jew-baiting, intellectual-baiting, and thought-controlling lynch-spirit." Yet this far from exhausts the list of unhappy or repulsive aberrations of the American spirit that have been attributed to Populism. Other aberrations are not pictured as a "seething mania" by any one critic, but by one or another the Populists are charged with some degree of responsibility for Anglophobia, Negrophobia, isolationism, imperialism, jingoism, paranoidal conspiracy-hunting, anti-Constitutionalism, anti-intellectualism, and the assault upon the right of privacy—these among others. The Populist virus is seen as no respecter of the barriers of time or nationality. According to Edward A. Shils, "populism has many faces. Nazi dictatorship had markedly populistic features. . . . Bolshevism has a strand of populism in it too." And there was among fellow travelers a "populistic predisposition to Stalinism." On the domestic scene the strand of Populistic tradition "is so powerful that it influences reactionaries like McCarthy and left-wing radicals and great upperclass personalities like Franklin Roosevelt." And according to Viereck, Populistic attitudes once "underlay Robespierre's Committee of Public Safety" and later "our neo-Populist Committee on un-American Activities."

Among certain of the critics there is no hesitancy in finding a direct continuity between the nineteenth-century Populists and twentieth-century American fascism and McCarthyism. Victor C. Ferkiss states flatly that "American fascism has its roots in American populism. It pursued the same ends and even used many of the same slogans. Both despaired of achieving a just society under the joined banners of liberalism and capitalism." His assertion supports Viereck's suggestion that "since the same impulses and resentments inspire the old Populism and the new nationalist right, let us adopt 'neo-Populism' as the proper term for the latter group." Talcott Parsons believes that "the elements of continuity between Western agrarian populism and McCarthyism are not by any means purely fortuitous," and Shils thinks the two are connected by "a straight line." It remains for Viereck to fill in the gap: "The missing link between the Populism of 1880–1900 and the neo-Populism of today—the missing link between Ignatius Donnelly and the McCarthy movement—was Father Charles Coughlin."

There is a strong tendency among the critics not only to identify Populism and the New Radical Right but to identify both with certain regions, the West and South, and particularly the Middle West. "The areas which produced the populism of the end of the nineteenth century and the early twentieth century have continued to produce them," writes Shils. Viereck puts it somewhat more colorfully: "The Bible-belt of Fundamentalism in religion mostly overlapped with the farm-belt of the Populist, Greenback, and other free-silver parties in politics. Both belts were anti-intellectual, anti-aristocratic, anti-capitalist." Parsons and Ferkiss likewise stress the regional identity of Populist-Radical Right ideology, and Viereck supplies an interesting illustration: "Out of the western Populist movement came such apostles of thought-control and racist bigotry as Tom Watson."

If so many undesirable traits are conveniently concentrated along geographical lines, it might serve a useful purpose to straighten out the political geography of Populism a bit. In the first place, as Hofstadter and other historians of the movement have noted, Populism had negligible appeal in the Middle Western states, and so did the quasi-

Populism of William Jennings Bryan. Wisconsin, Minnesota, Iowa, Illinois, and states east of them went down the line for William McKinley, Mark Hanna, gold, and the Old Conservatism (and so did Old Bob La Follette). Only in the plains states of North and South Dakota, Nebraska, and Kansas were there strong Populist leanings, and only they and the mountain states went for Bryan in 1896. At the crest of the Populist wave in 1894 only Nebraska polled a Populist vote comparable in strength to that run up in Alabama, Georgia, and North Carolina.

For the dubious distinction of being the leading Populist section, the South is in fact a strong contender; if the test used be merely quasi-Populism the pre-eminence of the former Confederacy is unchallengeable. It was easily the most solidly Bryan section of the country, and its dogged loyalty long outlasted that of the Nebraskan's native state. However, a more important test was third-party Populism, the genuine article. The remarkable strength the Populists manifested in the Lower South was gained against far more formidable obstacles than any ever encountered in the West. For there they daily faced the implacable dogmas of racism, white solidarity, white supremacy, and the bloody shirt. There was indeed plenty of "thought control and racist bigotry and lynch-spirit," but the Populists were far more often the victims than the perpetrators. They had to contend regularly with foreclosure of mortgages, discharge from jobs, eviction as tenants, exclusion from church, withholding of credit, boycott, social ostracism, and the endlessly reiterated charge of racial disloyalty and sectional disloyalty. Suspicion of loyalty was in fact *the* major psychological problem of the Southern Populists, as much so perhaps as the problem of loyalty faced by radicals of today. They contended also against cynical use of fraud comparable with any used against Reconstruction, methods that included stuffed ballot boxes, packed courts, stacked registration and election boards, and open bribery. They saw election after election stolen from them and heard their opponents boast of the theft. They were victims of mobs and lynchers. Some fifteen Negroes and several white men were killed in the Georgia Populist campaign of 1892, and it was rare that a major election in the Lower South came off without casualties.

Having waged their revolt at such great cost, the Southern Populists were far less willing to compromise their principles than were their Western brethren. It was the Western Populists who planned and led the movement to sell out the party to the Silverites, and the Southern Populists who fought and resisted the drift to quasi-Populism. The Southerners were consistently more radical, more insistent upon their economic reforms, and more stubbornly unwilling to lose their party identity in the watered-down quasi-Populism of Bryan than were the Westerners.

There is some lack of understanding about *who* the Southern Populists were for and against, as well as *what* they were for and against. Edward Shils writes that the "economic and political feebleness and pretensions to breeding and culture" of the "older aristocratic ruling class" in the South provided "a fertile ground for populistic denunciation of the upper classes." Actually the Southern Populists directed their rebellion against the newer ruling class, the industrialists and businessmen of the New South, instead of the old planters. A few of the quasi-Populists like Ben Tillman did divert resentment to aristocrats like Wade Hampton. But the South was still a more deferential society than the rest of the country, and the Populists were as ready as the railroads and insurance companies to borrow the prestige and name of a great family. The names of the Populist officials in Virginia sounded like a roll call of colonial assemblies or Revolutionary founding fathers: Page, Cocke, Harrison, Beverley, Ruffin. There were none more aristocratic in the Old Dominion. General Robert E. Lee, after the surrender at Appomattox, retired to the ancestral home of Edmund Randolph Cocke after his labors. His host was later Populist candidate for governor of the state. As the editor of their leading paper, the allegedly anglophobic Populists of Virginia chose Charles H. Pierson, an ordained Anglican priest, English by birth, Cambridge graduate, and theological student of Oxford. To be sure, the Populist leaders of Virginia were not typical of the movement in the South. But neither were Jefferson, Madison, Monroe, and John Taylor typical of *their* movement in the South: there were simply never enough aristocrats to go around. Some states had to make do with cruder customers as leaders in both Jeffersonian and Populist movements, and in the states to the west there was doubtless less habitual dependence on aristocrats, even if they had been more readily available.

In their analysis of the radical right of modern America, the new critics have made use of the concept of "status resentment" as the political motivation of their subjects.

They distinguish between "class politics," which has to do with the correction of economic deprivations, and "status politics," which has no definite solutions and no clear-cut legislative program but responds to irrational appeals and vents aggression and resentment for status insecurity upon scapegoats—usually ethnic minorities. Seymour Martin Lipset, who appears at times to include Populism in the category, has outlined the conditions typical of periods when status politics become ascendant. These are, he writes, "periods of prosperity, especially when full employment is accompanied by inflation, and when many individuals are able to improve their economic position." But the conditions under which Populism rose were exactly the opposite: severe depression, critical unemployment, and crippling currency contraction, when few were able to improve their economic position—and certainly not farmers in a cash-crop staple agriculture.

The Populist may have been bitten by status anxieties, but if so, they were certainly not bred of upward social mobility, and probably few by downward mobility either—for the simple reason that there was not much further downward for most Populists to go, and had not been for some time. Populism was hardly "status politics," and I should hesitate to call it "class politics." It was more nearly "interest politics," and more specifically "agricultural interest politics." Whatever concern the farmers might have had for their status was overwhelmed by desperate and immediate economic anxieties. Not only their anxieties but their proposed solutions and remedies were economic. While their legislative program may have often been naïve and inadequate, it was almost obsessively economic and, as political platforms go, little more irrational than the run-of-the-mill.

Yet one of the most serious charges leveled against the Populists in the reassessment of the new critics is an addiction to just the sort of irrational obsession that is typical of status politics. This is the charge of anti-Semitism. It has been documented most fully by Richard Hofstadter and Oscar Handlin and advanced less critically by others. The prejudice is attributed to characteristic Populist traits—rural provinciality, an ominous credulity, and an obsessive fascination with conspiracy. Baffled by the complexities of monetary and banking problems, Populist ideologues simplified them into a rural melodrama with Jewish international bankers as the principal villains. Numerous writings of Western Populists are cited that illustrate the tendency to use Jewish financiers and their race as scape-goats for agrarian resentment. Hofstadter points out that Populist anti-Semitism was entirely verbal and rhetorical and cautions that it can easily be misconstrued and exaggerated. He is nevertheless of the opinion "that the Greenback-Populist tradition activated most of what we have of modern popular anti-Semitism in the United States."

In the voluminous literature of the nineties on currency and monetary problems—problems that were much more stressed by silverites and quasi-Populists than by radical Populists—three symbols were repetitively used for the plutocratic adversary. One was institutional, "Wall Street," and two were ethnic, the British and Jewish bankers. Wall Street was by far the most popular and has remained so ever since among politicians of agrarian and Populistic tradition. Populist agitators used the ethnic symbols more or less indiscriminately, British along with Jewish, though some of them bore down with peculiar viciousness on the Semitic symbol. As the new critics have pointed out, certain Eastern intellectuals of the patrician sort, such as Henry and Brooks Adams and Henry Cabot Lodge, shared the Populist suspicion and disdain of the plutocracy and likewise shared their rhetorical anti-Semitism. John Higham has called attention to a third anti-Semitic group of the nineties, the poorer classes in urban centers. Their prejudice cannot be described as merely verbal and rhetorical. Populists were not responsible for a protest signed by fourteen Jewish societies in 1899 that "no Jew can go on the street without exposing himself to the danger of being pitilessly beaten." That happened in Brooklyn, and the mob of 1902 that injured some two hundred people, mostly Jewish, went into action in Lower East Side New York.

Populist anti-Semitism is not to be excused on the ground that it was verbal, nor dismissed because the prejudice received more violent expression in urban quarters. But all will admit that the charge of anti-Semitism has taken on an infinitely more ominous and hideous significance since the Nazi genocide furnaces than it ever had before, at least in Anglo-American society. The Populists' use of the Shylock symbol was not wholly innocent, but they used it as a folk stereotype, and little had happened in the Anglo-Saxon community between the time of Shakespeare and that of the Populists which burdened the latter with additional guilt in repeating the stereotype.

The South, again, was a special instance. Much had happened there to enhance the guilt of racist propaganda and to exacerbate racism. But anti-Semitism was not the trouble, and to stress it in connection with the South of the nineties would be comparable to stressing anti-Negro feeling in the Arab states of the Middle East today. Racism there was, in alarming quantity, but it was directed against another race, and it was not merely rhetorical. The Negro suffered far more discrimination and violence than the Jew did in that era or later. Moreover, there was little in the Southern tradition to restrain the political exploitation of anti-Negro prejudice and much more to encourage its use than there was in the American tradition with respect to anti-Semitism. Racism was exploited in the South with fantastic refinements and revolting excesses in the Populist period. Modern students of the dynamics of race prejudice find marked similarities between anti-Negro feelings and anti-Semitism and in the psychological traits of those to whom both appeal. First in the list of those traits under both anti-Negro attitudes and anti-Semitism is "the feeling of deprivation"; another, lower in the list but common to both, is "economic apprehensions." The Southern Populists would seem to have constituted the perfect market for Negrophobia.

But perhaps the most remarkable aspect of the whole Populist movement was the resistance its leaders in the South put up against racism and racist propaganda and the determined effort they made against incredible odds to win back political rights for the Negroes, defend those rights against brutal aggression, and create among their normally anti-Negro following, even temporarily, a spirit of tolerance in which the two races of the South could work together in one party for the achievement of common ends. These efforts included not only the defense of the Negro's right to vote but also his right to hold office, serve on juries, receive justice in the courts and defense against lynchers. The Populists failed, and some of them turned bitterly against the Negro as the cause of their failure. But in the efforts they made for racial justice and political rights they went further toward extending the Negro political fellowship, recognition, and equality than any native white political movement has ever gone before or since in the South. This record is of greater historical significance and deserves more emphasis and attention than any anti-Semitic tendencies the movement manifested in that region or any other. If resistance to racism is the test of acceptability for a place in the American political heritage, Populism would seem to deserve more indulgence at the hands of its critics than it has recently enjoyed.

Two other aspects of identification between the old Populism and the New Radical Right require critical modification. Talcott Parsons, Max Lerner, and Victor Ferkiss, among others, find that the old regional strongholds of Populism tended to become the strongholds of isolationism in the period between the two world wars and believe there is more than a fortuitous connection between a regional proneness to Populism and isolationism. These and other critics believe also that they discern a logical connection between a regional addiction to Populism in the old days and to McCarthyism in recent times.

In both of these hypotheses the critics have neglected to take into account the experience of the South and mistakenly assumed a strong Populist heritage in the Middle West. Although one of the strongest centers of Populism, if not the strongest, the South in the foreign policy crisis before the Second World War was the least isolationist and the most internationalist and interventionist part of the country. After the war, according to Nathan Glazer and Seymour Lipset, who base their statement on opinion poll studies, "the South was the most anti-McCarthy section of the country." It is perfectly possible that in rejecting isolationism and McCarthyism the South was "right" for the "wrong" reasons, traditional and historical reasons. V. O. Key has suggested that among the reasons for its position on foreign policy were centuries of dependence on world trade, the absence of any concentration of Irish or Germanic population, and the predominantly British origin of the white population. Any adequate explanation of the South's rejection of McCarthy would be complex, but part of it might be the region's peculiarly rich historical experience with its own assortment of demagogues—Populistic and other varieties—and the consequent acquirement of some degree of sophistication and some minimal standards of decency in the arts of demagoguery. No one has attempted to explain the South's anti-isolationism and anti-McCarthyism by reference to its Populist heritage—and certainly no such explanation is advanced here.

To do justice to the new critique of Populism it should be acknowledged that much of its bill of indictment is justified. It is true that the Populists were a provincial lot and that much of their thinking was provincial. It is true that they took refuge in the agrarian myth, that they denied the commercial character of agricultural enterprise and sometimes dreamed of a Golden Age. In their economic thought they overemphasized the importance of money and oversimplified the nature of their problems by claiming a harmony of interest between farmer and labor, by dividing the world into "producers" and "nonproducers," by reducing all conflict to "just two sides," and by thinking that too many ills and too many remedies of the world were purely legislative. Undoubtedly many of them were fascinated with the notion of conspiracy and advanced conspiratorial theories of history, and some of them were given to apocalyptic premonitions of direful portent.

To place these characteristics in perspective, however, one should enquire how many of them are peculiar to the Populists and how many are shared by the classes, or groups, or regions, or by the period to which the Populists belong. The great majority of Populists were provincial, ill-educated, and rural, but so were the great majority of Americans in the nineties, Republicans and Democrats as well. They were heir to all the superstition, folklore, and prejudice that is the heritage of the ill-informed. The Populists utilized and institutionalized some of this, but so did their opponents. There were a good many conspiratorial theories, economic nostrums, and oversimplifications adrift in the latter part of the nineteenth century, and the Populists had no monopoly of them. They did overemphasize the importance of money, but scarcely more so than did their opponents, the Gold Bugs. The preoccupation with monetary reforms and remedies was a characteristic of the period rather than a peculiarity of the Populists. The genuine Populist, moreover, was more concerned with the "primacy of credit" than with the "primacy of money," and his insistence that the federal government was the only agency powerful enough to provide a solution for the agricultural credit problem proved to be sound. So did his contention that the banking system was stacked against his interest and that reform in this field was overdue.

The Populist doctrine of a harmony of interest between farmer and labor, between workers and small businessmen, and the alignment of these "producers" against the parasitic "nonproducers" is not without precedent in our political history. Any party that aspires to gain power in America must strive for a coalition of conflicting interest groups. The Populist effort was no more irrational in this respect than was the Whig coalition and many others, including the New Deal.

The political crises of the nineties evoked hysterical responses and apocalyptic delusions in more than one quarter. Excesses of the leaders of a protest movement of provincial, unlettered, and angry farmers are actually more excusable and understandable than the rather similar responses of the spokesmen of the educated, successful, and privileged classes of the urban East. There would seem to be less excuse for hysteria and conspiratorial obsessions among the latter. One thinks of the *Nation* describing the

Sherman Silver Purchase Act as a "socialistic contrivance of gigantic proportions," of J. Laurence Laughlin writing of "the great silver conspiracy" in the *Atlantic Monthly* of 1896, or of Police Commissioner Theodore Roosevelt declaring in "the greatest soberness" that the Populists were "plotting a social revolution and the subversion of the American Republic" and proposing to make an example of twelve of their leaders by "shooting them dead" against a wall. There was Joseph H. Choate before the Supreme Court pronouncing the income tax "the beginnings of socialism and communism" and "the destruction of the Constitution itself." For violence of rhetoric *Harper's Weekly*, the *Atlantic Monthly,* the New York *Tribune,* and the Springfield *Republican* could hold their own with the wool-hat press in the campaign of 1896. Hysteria was not confined to mugwump intellectuals with status problems. Mark Hanna told an assembly of his wealthy friends at the Union League Club they were acting like "a lot of scared hens."

Anarchism was almost as much a conspiracy symbol for conservatives as Wall Street was for the Populists, and conservatives responded to any waving of the symbol even more irrationally, for there was less reality in the menace of anarchism for capitalism. John Hay had a vituperative address called "The Platform of Anarchy" that he used in the campaign of 1896. The Springfield *Republican* called Bryan "the exaltation of anarchy"; Dr. Lyman Abbott labeled Bryanites "the anarchists of the Northwest," and Dr. Charles H. Parkhurst was excited about the menace of "anarchism" in the Democratic platform. It was the

Populist sympathizer, Governor John Peter Altgeld of Illinois, who pardoned the three anarchists of Haymarket, victims of conservative hysteria, and who partly corrected the gross miscarriage of justice that had resulted in the hanging of four others. The New York *Times* promptly denounced Governor Altgeld as a secret anarchist himself, and Theodore Roosevelt said that Altgeld would conspire to inaugurate "a red government of lawlessness and dishonesty as fantastic and vicious as the Paris Commune." There was more than a touch of conspiratorial ideology in the desperate conservative reaction to the agrarian revolt. An intensive study of the nineties can hardly fail to leave the impression that this decade had rather more than its share of zaniness and crankiness and that these qualities were manifested in the higher and middling as well as the lower orders of American society.

Venturing beyond the 1890's and speaking of populists with a small "p," some of the new critics would suggest that popular protest movements of the populistic style throughout our history have suffered from a peculiar addiction to scares, scapegoats, and conspiratorial notions. It is true that such movements tend to attract the less sophisticated, the people who are likely to succumb to cranks and the appeal of their menaces, and conspiratorial obsessions. But before one accepts this as a populistic or radical peculiarity, one should recall that the Jacobin Scare of the 1790's was a Federalist crusade and that the populistic elements of that era were its victims and not its perpetrators. One should remember also that A. Mitchell Palmer and the superpatriots who staged the Great Red Scare of 1919–1920

were not populistic in their outlook. One of the most successful conspiratorial theories of history in American politics was the "Great Slave Conspiracy" notion advanced by
the abolitionists and later incorporated in the Republican
party credo for several decades.

Richard Hofstadter has put his finger on a neglected
tendency of some Populists and Progressives as well, the
tendency he calls "deconversion from reform to reaction,"
the tendency to turn cranky, illiberal, and sour. This happened with disturbing frequency among leaders as well as
followers of Populism. Perhaps the classic example is the
Georgia Populist, Tom Watson, twice his party's candidate
for President and once for Vice President. When Watson
soured he went the whole way. By no means all of the
Populist leaders turned sour, and there has been an over-
emphasis on a handful of stock examples, but there are
several valid instances. Even more disturbing is the same
tendency to turn sour among the old Populist rank and file,
to take off after race phobias, religious hatreds, and witch
hunts. The reasons for this retrograde tendency among reformers to embrace the forces they have spent years in
fighting have not been sufficiently investigated. It may be
that in some instances the reform movement appeals to
personalities with unstable psychological traits. In the case
of the Populists, however, it would seem that a very large
part of the explanation lies in embittered frustration—
repeated and tormenting frustration of both the leaders
and the led.

Whatever the explanation, it cannot be denied that some
of the offshoots of Populism are less than lovely to con-

template and rather painful to recall. Misshapen and sometimes hideous, they are caricatures of the Populist ideal, though their kinship with the genuine article is undeniable. No one in his right mind can glory in their memory, and it would at times be a welcome relief to renounce the whole Populist heritage in order to be rid of the repulsive aftermath. Repudiation of the Populist tradition presents the liberal-minded Southerner in particular with a temptation of no inconsiderable appeal, for it would unburden him of a number of embarrassing associations.

In his study of populist traits in American society, Edward Shils has some perceptive observations on the difficult relations between politicians and intellectuals. He adds a rather wistful footnote: "How painful the American situation looked to our intellectuals when they thought of Great Britain. There the cream of the graduates of the two ancient universities entered the civil service by examinations which were delightfully archaic and which had no trace of spoils patronage about them. . . . Politics, radical politics, conducted in a seemly fashion by the learned and reflective was wonderful. It was an ideal condition which was regretfully recognized as impossible to reproduce in the United States." He himself points out many of the reasons why this is possible in Britain, the most dignified member of the parliamentary fraternity: respect for "betters," mutual trust within the ruling classes, deferential attitudes of working class and middle class, the aura of aristocracy and monarchy that still suffuses the institutions of a government no longer aristocratic, the retention of the status and the symbols of hierarchy despite economic leveling. No wonder that from some points of view "the British system seemed an intellectual's paradise."

America has it worse—or at least different. The deferential attitude lingers only in the South, and there mainly as a quaint gesture of habit. Respect for "betters" is un-American. Glaring publicity replaces mutual trust as the *modus vivendi* among the political elite. No aura of aristocratic decorum and hierarchal sanctity surrounds our governmental institutions, even the most august of them. Neither Supreme Court nor State Department nor Army is immune from popular assault and the rude hand of suspicion. The sense of institutional identity is weak, and so are institutional loyalties. Avenues between the seats of learning and the seats of power are often blocked by mistrust and mutual embarrassment.

America has no reason to expect that it could bring off a social revolution without a breach of decorum or the public peace, nor that the revolutionary party would eventually be led by a graduate of exclusive Winchester and Oxford. American politics are not ordinarily "conducted in a seemly fashion by the learned and reflective." Such success as we have enjoyed in this respect—the instances of the Sage of Monticello and the aristocrat of Hyde Park come to mind—have to be accounted for by a large element of luck. Close investigation of popular upheavals of protest and reform in the political history of the United States has increasingly revealed of late that they have all had their seamy side and their share of the irrational, the zany, and the retrograde. A few of the more successful movements have borrowed historical reputability from the memory of the worthies who led them, but others have not been so fortunate either in their leaders or their historians.

One must expect and even hope that there will be future upheavals to shock the seats of power and privilege and furnish the periodic therapy that seems necessary to the health of our democracy. But one cannot expect them to be any more decorous or seemly or rational than their predecessors. One can reasonably hope, however, that they will not all fall under the sway of the Huey Longs and Father Coughlins who will be ready to take charge. Nor need they, if the tradition is maintained which enabled a Henry George to place himself at the vanguard of the antimonopoly movement in his day, which encouraged a Henry Demarest Lloyd to labor valiantly to shape the course of Populism, or which prompted an Upton Sinclair to try to make sense of a rag-tag-and-bob-tail aberration in California.

For the tradition to endure, for the way to remain open, however, the intellectual must not be alienated from the sources of revolt. It was one of the glories of the New Deal that it won the support of the intellectual and one of the tragedies of Populism that it did not. The intellectual must resist the impulse to identify all the irrational and evil forces he detests with such movements because some of them, or the aftermath or epigone of some of them, have proved so utterly repulsive. He will learn all he can from the new criticism about the irrational and illiberal side of Populism and other reform movements, but he cannot afford to repudiate the heritage.

8

What Happened to the Civil Rights Movement

STUDENTS OF NEGRO LIFE IN AMERICA HAVE ENJOYED some rare opportunities during recent years. As if adopting the techniques of the cinema director, history has obligingly thrown in a succession of flashbacks or replays of hauntingly familiar lines, encounters, whole episodes from the past. It would seem at times, in fact, that contemporary history has been plagiarizing an old scenario and helping itself to the script.

With all due resistance to superficial parallels, we have been unable to avoid comparisons between past history and lived experience. For we have witnessed in our own time a rising tide of indignation against an ancient wrong, the slow crumbling of stubborn resistance, the sudden rush and elation of victory, and then the onset of reaction and the fading of high hopes.

I

We remember how both political parties long resisted identification with the new movement, as they did once before, and how one of them became reluctantly involved, then slowly veered toward commitment. Beginning timidly with half measures and cautious concessions, Congress gradually closed the gap between its own mood and that of the more radical Supreme Court, which had all along blazed the trail and set the pace. One new civil rights bill then followed another, each bolder and more aggressive than the last: 1957, 1960, 1964, 1965. Sweeping, comprehensive statutes, they promised the oppressed emancipation from the bonds of segregation and discrimination, and protection of civil rights, restoration of the franchise and political rights, and broadened opportunities for education and economic advancement.

The drama unfolded on a familiar stage, with scenes employing old settings—federal, state, and local. The new cast of actors mouthed the old lines and rattled the old stage swords of Constitutional polemics. There were the inevitable confrontations: North with South, black with white, federal power with state rights, judiciary with legislative branch, executive with the other two, true believer with skeptic, Northern missionary with harsh reality, Southern paternalist with alienated beneficiary. They were the classic encounters, the traditional roles of the First Reconstruction.

It would be a simple exercise to elaborate the analogies and spin out the parallels, but the differences are more impressive than the similarities. Perhaps it was because this time we were spectators as well as students of events, because one could sometimes say, "I was there." For we were all involved in some measure and could stake some claim to it as *our* movement, at least in the sense that it was the greatest social movement of our time. Whether for these reasons or less subjective ones, "our" movement does seem unmatched in many respects by its historic counterpart of the last century.

For one thing there is no doubt about the comparative numbers involved, both absolute and relative, both black and white. It is harder to compare involvement of the Negroes fairly, for in the 1860's their participation was hardly a matter of choice. As for the whites, apart from the strictly military aspects, those of the 1960's were proportionately more widely engaged. Certainly more parts, in fact nearly all parts, of the country were involved this time, for it was no longer a movement inflicted by one part of the country upon another. It was for a time, but it did not remain that. I am not at all sure about the religious community, but it is plain that the intellectual community, and more particularly the academic community, was far more committed this time than last. I would not venture a comparison of the relative depth of dedication, but the best estimate is a maximum of five thousand Yankee schoolmarms in the South. They probably had more staying power than their twentieth century counterparts, but they hardly rivaled their numbers if summer recruits, marchers, and freedom-riders be included.

Pushing comparisons beyond those of numbers is more hazardous. But for what it is worth, I think there are strong contrasts in style, temper, and rhythm. These are due in large measure to two distinctive features of the Second Reconstruction: (1) the predominance of the

Negro, and (2) the predominance of youth. This helps explain why it was more spontaneous and less contrived, more improvised and less premeditated. It had a wild, untamed exuberance baffling to the older generation. Paternalists and philanthropists of the establishment, black and white, not only lost control, they often lost touch. They were not *with* it. In the theme song of the revolution the verb "overcome" was intransitive, but had it taken the transitive form, one of the objects of "to overcome" would have been "the older generation." For this was in part a generational rebellion that cut across racial lines and transcended racial objectives. Retirement age for leaders of this wing seems to be about twenty-six, and there is already a substantial list of emeriti.

Youth was one distinctive and appealing aspect of the movement. Suddenly shedding the "mark of oppression" that was supposed to deprive them of initiative and paralyze them for action, the children of oppression impulsively took to the streets with the cry of Freedom Now. They sprang to the vanguard, furnished the martyrs, produced the heroes. A hundred scenes come to mind: kids marching into schools through the gauntlets of hostile, spitting, screaming white parents; the four teen-age freshmen of the Greensboro college taking their seats at the Woolworth lunch counter, silently enduring indignities and launching the sit-in movement; the great student demonstrations through the streets of the hard-core white supremacy cities, facing police dogs, fire hose, tear gas; and always the singing, singing in the streets, singing in the jails. I wonder if there has been anything quite like it since the Middle Ages. There was certainly nothing like it in the First Reconstruction.

Nor was there anything in the 1860's that quite lived up to the sheer drama of the great climactic moments of recent years—the classic presidential performances, one set of them reminiscent of another miscast general; another in clipped, Bostonian accents; a third in the evangelical rhetoric of Texas. Other roles were filled by incomparable performers—the mass leaders, the orators, the singers. And where could one find more satisfactory villains than Bull Connor and Sheriff Jim Clark?

No one who witnessed them or took part in them will ever forget the great mass demonstrations and marches. Beside them Coxey's Army and the Bonus Army fade into insignificance, for nothing comparable ever happened before in our history. Two hundred thousand strong the Marchers on Washington stood before Father Abraham, listened to Mahalia Jackson belt out her heart in song, and hung on Martin Luther King's lyrical refrain, "I have a dream." Those are unforgettable moments. And so also are the climactic scenes of the march from Selma to Montgomery, the massed thousands packed in the square facing the old capitol of the Confederacy. And again the songs, the oratory, the soaring hopes, and the generous, heart-pounding emotions.

2

All those stirring events were quite recent, so recent that the sound of them was still in our ears. And yet they seemed at the same time so remote, so improbable. For who can quite imagine now another Mississippi Summer, another Selma, another joint session of Congress rising to give a standing ovation to a President who intoned, "We shall overcome," or the same President or another intoning it again?

Historians have their armchair consolations, of course, their after-dinner ironies with brandy. We knew all along, or so we inform the young and ill tutored, that all revolutionary upheavals have their life cycle: rise, climax, decline, reaction. There were the numerous precedents and the relevant monographs. We knew too well—and the knowledge always rather embarrassed encounters with true believers—that high fevers of idealism and soaring moods of self-sacrifice cannot be sustained indefinitely, that they lag and burn themselves out, that disenchantment and self-doubt eventually set in. And one could expect from past experience that extremists at both ends would take over and make common cause against the rational mean. Then come the men of the last act who recite their traditional lines: that reforms have proceeded too fast, that violence and disorder have gone too far, that extremists must be got in hand, and that law and order must be established at all costs.

It may be that in due course, say on the eve of the Third Reconstruction, some enterprising historian will bring out a monograph on the Compromise that ended the Second Reconstruction, entitled perhaps *The Triumph of Tokenism*. And he may judiciously set forth the background of how the people wearied of the annual August ghetto riots and the inevitable call for troops, of the farcical war on poverty and all the corruption and the squandering of public funds, of the rise of racist demagogues, black and white, and their shameless antics in New York, Baltimore, Atlanta, and Los Angeles. And he will write of how conservatives of North and South, East and West came together regardless of party and called a halt, and how Negro leaders were divided in council and fell out with each other, and how their white allies withdrew in silence and confusion and timidity, and how some of them and some of their Negro friends tacitly acquiesced in the consensus of tokenism, and how a few took high office and endorsed it. Then, observing that since in the first instance the cycle ran from 1865 to 1877 and in the second from 1954 to 1966, our future historian may tentatively hypothesize that a baker's dozen years is par for the course.

I hasten to add that I am not the future historian, that I do not buy his glib structure of causation, that I reject his spurious analogies, and that I am not about to endorse his periodization or his cheap fatalism. In fact I am not a determinist of any sort.

Reaction had set in, of course—call it backlash or frontlash. No doubt about that. But the conventional explanations centering on the Black Power movement and the black ghetto riots did not really explain, did not ring true. After all, Malcolm X had been effectively disseminating all the Black Power racist dogmas for years through the most radical phases of the movement, and the popular response was more white radicalism instead of reaction. The ghetto riots were certainly no help, but before settling on them as the cause of the reaction of '66 it might be recalled that the first summer of riots was followed by the landslide of '64 and some of the most radical phases of the revolution, including the Selma-Montgomery March and the Voting Rights Act of '65.

Coupling 1966 with 1877 is calculated to produce other shudders in the historian's nervous system. There existed no such dramatic bargaining opportunities as there were in 1877. Furthermore, this time any bargaining table would have had to reserve a place for a more or less responsible spokesman of the Negroes themselves. But merely to mention 1877 is to conjure up the horrors of the great freeze that set in that year and lasted until the great thaw of recent times. It was marked by the repudiation or nullification of virtually the entire body of law accumulated over the revolutionary decade preceding in so far as this offered federal and required state protection of Negro rights, and a thoroughgoing betrayal of whatever idealism the Civil War embodied save the elementary outlawing of slavery. It is simply inconceivable that such an appalling reversal of history could be repeated.

Nevertheless, after all that is admitted and underlined, it should never be used to dismiss the importance or diminish the significance of what happened in 1966. For however future historians may explain it and whatever consequences they may attribute to it, we know that 1966 —call it watershed or turning point—was a critical year in our history. The evidence was all around us. More came in constantly from far and wide, East Coast, West Coast, Midwest, and South. Scarcely a city of any size failed to reflect it, and rarely did a politician fail to respond. It ran through pages of congressional debates and in and out of policy decisions.

Federal agencies charged with the enforcement of the sweeping provisions of the new civil rights acts suddenly found their appropriations jeopardized, their guidelines attacked, their orders brushed aside, and their officers demoralized. "We accepted tokenism," said a spokesman of the Department of Justice. "What more do they want?"

Intimations of what more was wanted were to be found in determined assaults in Congress on Title VI of the Civil Rights Act of 1964 authorizing the withholding of federal funds on account of racial discrimination in government-assisted programs. Once called "the atomic bomb of civil rights," Title VI came within inches of being defused. The assault, according to a spokesman of the Department of Health, Education and Welfare, was "making a difficult enforcement task even harder." The Senate attempted to let local physicians decide when patients could be segregated in hospitals for health reasons. The House threatened to require hearings in advance of any move to withhold funds from school districts suspected of discrimination. Other congressional actions menaced salaries, reduced personnel, and impugned the motives of enforcement agencies.

From the rest of the country came mainly silence or consent. "Everywhere you look with people in position of power and authority," observed Leslie Dunbar, a foundation executive, "they have things they regard as more important." Foreign crises to be solved, inflation to be curbed, elections to be won. Leaders of the Jewish community were worried about the anti-Semitism of Negro extremists. Negro leaders were divided among themselves, and their followers milled in confusion. White liberals and the New Left thought Vietnam was more important and choked a bit on the Black Power slogan. Labor leaders and politicians were concerned about their "image." And over the college campus the civil rights trumpet made an uncertain sound, or none at all. Lately embattled students carried new placards or returned to their books. A great stillness descended upon quarters long noted for outspoken opinions.

How long the trend of reaction would last and when the tide would turn we had no means of knowing. But we do know that we no longer live in the same moral, political, and intellectual climate to which we have accustomed ourselves in the period of ten or twelve years recently ended. And if we are realists we will no longer pretend that the movement for racial justice and Negro rights is sustained by the same foundation of moral assurance, or that it is supported any longer by the same political coalitions, the same interracial accommodations, and such harmony of purpose, commitment, and dedication as had once prevailed.

To call this a passing "phase," an interruption of a continuous movement, is to miss the historic integrity and distinctiveness of the recent period. It was a period of restitution, an effort to fulfill promises a century old, the redemption of a historic commitment. The appeal to history touched the Great Emancipator's "mystic chords of memory" and evoked a crusading mood charged with romantic sentiment. It was in that mood that the mass marches ("black and white together") were conducted. The objectives were clear and simple and the struggle for fulfillment took place largely in the South, the proper historic (and properly remote) setting for reconstructions. The last major milestone of the crusade was the Voting Rights Act of 1965.

Even before that event, however, problems of a new and disturbingly different character were demanding attention—things like slums, housing, unemployment, deteriorating school and family, delinquency, and riots. They were not wrapped in historic sanctions and they were not amenable to romantic crusades and the evangelical approach. They were tough and harsh and brutally raw. What's more, they were national problems, not Southern, though the South faced some of them too. As soon as this came home to the North the great withdrawal set in. White congressmen from the Bronx and Chicago set up cries of anguish and dismay as bitter as the familiar chorus from South Carolina and Mississippi. Amid the clamor (North and South together) the Civil Rights Bill of 1966 for open housing and protection of civil rights workers (combining "Northern" and "Southern" issues) went down in crashing defeat.

How long before the country would be prepared to face up to a Third Reconstruction—which is what a realistic solution of the new national problems really amounted to —remained to be seen. And whether much of the spent momentum and the old élan of past crusades would be marshaled and how many veteran leaders could be enlisted to get an entirely new program off the ground was problematical. The White House Conference of June, 1966, which was designed to do just these things, failed of its purpose. Whites and blacks share some of the blame. But public attention was diverted elsewhere. Foreign wars are notorious distractors of public attention—especially when people *want* to be distracted. Veterans of the Second Reconstruction and planners of a Third would do well to face up to the fact that the one is now over and the other is still struggling to be born.

The unhappy interlude, which may be prolonged, would seem an appropriate time for reflection on the remarkable experience through which we have lately passed and such lessons as it might have to teach. In the past whenever one of these hurricanes of indignation, righteousness, guilt, impatience, or whatever swept the country, it left things in a state of disarray. The winds came in alternate gusts of love and hate and they left nothing undisturbed. It happened thus in the storm over slavery, and the latest tempest, while not so bloody, has had its effect. An inventory of our mental furniture will bear this out.

3

The history of the American intellectual community is beset with violent love affairs with other classes. Those of a certain age will be able to recall the one of the thirties.

That one was conducted across class lines and its object was the workingman, but its course was quite as tempestuous as the more recent affair. Such affairs of the heart have been in the romantic tradition that endows the object of love with exalted virtues and sublime attributes and at the same time indulges the lover in dreams of glory and self-flattery.

The passion was manifest in different forms. The white Southerner, his ardor and devotion suspect from the start, was most given to violent protestation and self-abasement. But in action he was prone to lapse unconsciously into hereditary postures of benevolent paternalism. The white Northerner, the more confident and masterful suitor, was not immune from hereditary posturing himself, and could set forth on his freedom ride humming the "Battle Hymn of the Republic." The Negro intellectual, cast in the curious role of both lover and beloved, was subjected to all the temptations of narcissism and occasionally succumbed. Some of the whites, overcome with conviction of communal guilt, succumbed to impulses of masochism and begged nothing of the beloved but to be publicly whipped and generally abused. And for a suitable fee there were those who were ready to oblige from the platform, the stage, or the screen.

These impulses, however, were but deviations from the white norm of neo-paternalism, a compound of philanthropy and unconscious condescension. For the underlying assumption was that it was up to the white man to solve "the problem," to lift up the black brother, to redeem the Negro. An incidental dividend that the

philanthropist sometimes demanded of the freedom
march or the jail-in was an ennobling catharsis. So pro-
miscuous was the resulting role confusion that it was hard
to say at times whether the actor was playing redeemer
or redeemed, or whether the underlying purpose of a
particular march or freedom school was black salvation
or white.

The picture was further complicated by the exalted
roles the white romantics assigned their black partners.
In effect they turned the tables of racial dogma and opted
for Negro supremacy. But it was a dubious brand of
supremacy, and the flattery, as Robert Penn Warren has
pointed out, was shot through with the condescension implicit in the eighteenth-century adoration of the Noble
Savage. The savage was extravagantly praised and admired, but he was admired for very particular kinds of
virtues. They were the virtues attributed to the natural
man, the simple child of nature, untainted by the malaise
of civilization and untrammeled by its inhibitions, its compromises, and its instinctual deprivations. The modern
Negro, like the Noble Savage, was endowed with the
compensatory graces of simplicity, naturalness, spontane-
ity, and uninhibited sexuality.

The white Southerner, even the more orthodox of the
breed, has long been familiar with this projection of
yearnings and the type of condescension involved. They
have haunted daydreams down the generations and provide the central theme of hundreds of pious folk stories,
and some not so pious. They range in degree of sophistication from the legendary virtues of black mammy and

the fabulous lubricity of black folk generally to dreams of restored innocence based on the literary model of Huck Finn and Nigger Jim: "Come back to the raft, Huck, honey."

The Yankees came to this exercise with a fresher approach. The red man as the Noble Savage of an earlier day and Uncle Tom as an abolitionist projection were far behind them, and the rediscovery of the Negro opened fresh challenges to the imagination. They embraced him with an impulsiveness and fervor that must have proved embarrassing to the Negro at times. Another turning of the tables seems to have endowed the whites with the gift for imitation traditionally attributed to the blacks, and made the latter the object of the most abject cultural imitation of modern times. Whites assiduously cultivated Negro slang, Negro music, Negro dance, Negro postures, Negro attitudes—or at least the slang, music, dance, postures, and attitudes they fondly attributed to the Negro.

Jazz and gospel songs penetrated the concert halls and jive talk became the language of the avant-garde. The White Negro was a literary creation of the times, and one of the most incredible performances in that role was a London beat holding forth at Oxford in what he doubtless believed to be the true idiom of 125th Street. It was acculturation in reverse. It was Harlem replacing the Phillipsian plantation as a school for white savages manqués. What's more, it was dead serious, at least to the true believers. In their eyes the Negro was the spiritual salvation for a bankrupt white civilization that had lost its vital juices and was destined for the dumpheap of history.

The scholarly community was more reserved and less impulsive in its responses, but it did not remain unmoved. Its contributions were usually hedged with qualifications and cautious exceptions that were ignored by popularizers and propagandists. The historian was often shocked to read of the lessons his book allegedly taught and desperately sought to disavow them. But the disavowals rarely caught up with the lessons. Such hypotheses as the one that "innately Negroes *are,* after all, only white men with black skins, nothing more, nothing less" quickly acquired uses beyond the author's control. The chicken-and-egg argument over slave status and race prejudice—which came first and which caused which—took on a polemical edge and urgency far beyond the power of existing evidence to satisfy. To meet the needs of the Negro revolution evidence was tortured to yield support for a heroic legend of slave revolt, and the image of the abolitionist was burnished to a new brightness.

Comparisons of Anglo-American with Latin American slavery and race relations have legitimately raised questions about the relative benevolence of the homegrown institution. But the lesson-teachers and the moral-drawers, with a hot commodity for the guilt-and-contrition white market, were not content with suggestive hypotheses nor willing to wait for scholarly tests. One of them came forward confidently with the conclusion that "American slavery was profoundly different from, and in its lasting effects on individuals and their children, indescribably worse than, any recorded servitude, ancient or modern." Which took in a good deal of unexplored territory. And a sociologist thought the only remaining question was, "Why was American slavery the most awful the world has ever seen?"

Historians responded to the long evident need for revision of musty Reconstruction history with a copious flow of monographs, but the lessons the Second Reconstruction taught the historians of the First, and the lessons the First allegedly had for activists of the Second were sometimes garbled in transmission. One historian suggested that the full-blown system of legally enforced segregation was not an immediate sequel of Appomattox, only to find himself cited as authority for the doctrine that Jim Crow was superficially rooted and easily eradicated. And when he called attention to the union of Negroes and whites in Southern Populism, he was interpreted as prophesying millennial developments in politics. It is no news to teachers, of course, that the lessons taught are not always the lessons learned.

4

How Negro Americans have withstood with such poise and humor as they have the crises they have weathered is one of the greatest marvels of the whole period. When one takes into account the constant barrage of publicity— front-page headlines for a decade or more—plus the attention, flattery, and imitation of the faddists, plus the adulation and cagerness of the activists, it would seem enough to have turned the head of the whole race. Perhaps it was because all this was more than neutralized by the indifference, hatred, and brutality of the other whites. Or because of what Ralph Ellison has called the Negro's "tragicomic attitude toward the universe." At any rate it is clear that among the great majority of the leaders and the followers of the Negro movement the racial reserve of humor and sanity has never failed.

This cannot be said of a minority in whom the "tragicomic attitude" seems to have been in short supply. They have attracted an amount of attention disproportionate to their numbers because of a talent for making themselves conspicuous. Among them are the unfortunate few who have attempted to live up—or, rather, down—to the white myth of the Noble Savage, super-rhythm, super-lubricity and all. A smaller number have solemnly shouldered the new black man's burden—another white invention—of playing redeemer to a doomed white civilization.

More prominent are those who have elected to withdraw into some sort of racial exclusiveness, rejecting white allies and white society. Withdrawal takes several organized forms, including a cult of negritude, one that rallies to the cry of Black Power, and black nationalists of the Muslim and other varieties, all glorifying race and exalting racial identity. "A mystique must be created," reads a pronouncement of SNCC members which declares that "If we are to proceed toward true liberation, we must cut ourselves off from white people. We must form our own institutions, credit unions, co-ops, political parties, write our own histories." Like the pronouncements of other separatist groups, this has the unmistakable quality of fantasy and a tenuous contact with reality. That all but a few of the Negro leaders of national prominence have publicly repudiated this philosophy, along with any strategies of violence and racial exclusiveness and demagoguery, is one of a few reassuring signs of the time.

Any realistic appraisal of the prospects of the movement for Negro rights and a Third Reconstruction to come would take full account of the ominous signs of reaction mentioned earlier. This would include the numerous white defections from the commitment to racial justice, the sudden silence in many quarters recently vocal with protest, the mounting appeal to bigotry, and the scurry of retreat in Congress. If past experience is any guide, it would be the part of realism to expect things to get worse before they get even worse.

It would not be the part of realism, however, to omit from the appraisal such assets as remain. Foremost among these surely is a corps of experienced Negro leaders that has not been surpassed in dedication, astuteness, and moral force by the leadership of any other great social movement of this century. Their power is still great, and many of them have already enlisted for the Third Reconstruction. Although a smaller percentage of the Negroes now vote than voted in the First Reconstruction, their votes are more strategically located and more powerfully felt. While there may be further defections among the whites, a younger generation of blacks and whites that shares a powerful sense of identity with this movement and has made it peculiarly its own is coming on strong. It will be heard from further. Until its force is spent, there is no realism in accepting the current reaction as irreversible and no rationality in despair.

Postscript, April, 1968: The tragic loss of Martin Luther King necessarily modifies even the cautious words of optimism with which the above essay was concluded in November, 1966. It is true that as young as he was at the time of his death King was still more identified with the Second Reconstruction, which had largely run its course, than he had yet come to be with the Third Reconstruction, which was struggling to be born. For the last year or more of his life, however, he had been striving heroically to redirect his leadership from a Southern to a Northern or national orientation, from preoccupation with legal rights to a drive for economic objectives. His purpose was to embody the new aspirations and needs in his own rhetoric of nonviolence and hope and to resist their embodiment in the idiom of the ghetto, in the rhetoric of despair, aliena-tion, racism, and violence. Whether he would have suc-ceeded in his strivings we will never know.

9

The Irony of Southern History

IN A TIME WHEN NATIONALISM SWEEPS EVERYTHING ELSE before it, as it does at present, the regional historian is likely to be oppressed by a sense of his unimportance. America is the all-important subject, and national ideas, national institutions, and national policies are the themes that compel attention. Foreign peoples, eager to know what this New-World colossus means to them and their immediate future, are impatient with details of regional variations, and Americans, intent on the need for national unity, tend to minimize their importance. New England, the West, and other regions are occasionally permitted to speak for the nation. But the South is thought to be hedged about with peculiarities that set it apart as unique. As a standpoint from which to write American history it is regarded as eccentric and, as a background for an historian, something of a handicap to be overcome.

Of the eccentric position of the South in the nation there are admittedly many remaining indications. I do not think, however, that this eccentricity need be regarded as entirely a handicap. In fact, I think that it could possibly be turned to advantage by the Southern historian, both in understanding American history and in interpreting it to non-Americans. For from a broader point of view it is not the South but America that is unique among the peoples of the world. This peculiarity arises out of the American legend of success and victory, a legend that is not shared by any other people of the civilized world. The collective will of this country has simply never known what it means to be confronted by complete frustration. Whether by luck, by abundant resources, by ingenuity, by technology, by organizing cleverness, or by sheer force of arms America has been able to overcome every major historic crisis—economic, political, or foreign—with which it has had to cope. This remarkable record has naturally left a deep imprint upon the American mind. It explains in large part the national faith in unlimited progress, in the efficacy of material means, in the importance of mass and speed, the worship of success, and the belief in the invincibility of American arms.

The legend has been supported by an unbroken succession of victorious wars. Some were less victorious than others, but none was a defeat. In the course of their national history Americans, who have been called a bellicose though unmartial people, have fought eight wars, and so far without so much as one South African fiasco such as England encountered in the heyday of her power. This unique good fortune has isolated America, I think rather dangerously, from the common experience of the rest of mankind, all the great peoples of which have without exception known the bitter taste of defeat and humiliation. It has fostered the tacit conviction that American ideals, values, and principles inevitably prevail in the end. That conviction has never received a name, nor even so much explicit formulation as the old concept of Manifest Destiny. It is assumed, not discussed. And the assumption exposes us to the temptation of believing that we are somehow immune from the forces of history.

The country that has come nearest to approximating the American legend of success and victory is England. The nearness of continental rivals and the precariousness of the balance of power, however, bred in the English an historical sophistication that prevented the legend from flourishing as luxuriantly as it has in the American climate. Only briefly toward the end of the Victorian period did the legend threaten to get out of hand in England. Arnold J. Toynbee has recalled those piping days in a reminiscent passage. "I remember watching the Diamond Jubilee procession myself as a small boy," he writes. "I remember the atmosphere. It was: well, here we are on the top of the world, and we have arrived at this peak to stay there—forever! There is, of course, a thing called history, but history is something unpleasant that happens to other people. We are comfortably outside all that. I am sure, if I had been a small boy in New York in 1897 I should have felt the same. Of course, if I had been a small boy in 1897 in the Southern part of the United States, I should not have felt the same; I should then have known from my parents that history had happened to my people in my part of the world."

The South has had its full share of illusions, fantasies, and pretensions, and it has continued to cling to some of them with an astonishing tenacity that defies explanation. But the illusion that "history is something unpleasant that happens to other people" is certainly not one of them—not in the face of accumulated evidence and memory to the contrary. It is true that there have been many Southern converts to the gospel of progress and success, and there was even a period following Reconstruction when it seemed possible that these converts might carry a reluctant region with them. But the conversion was never anywhere near complete. Full participation in the legend of irresistible progress, success, and victory could, after all, only be vicarious at best. For the inescapable facts of history were that the South had repeatedly met with frustration and failure. It had learned what it was to be faced with economic, social, and political problems that refused to yield to all the ingenuity, patience, and intelligence that a people could bring to bear upon them. It had learned to accommodate itself to conditions that it swore it would never accept, and it had learned the taste left in the mouth by the swallowing of one's own words. It had learned to live for long decades in quite un-American poverty, and it had learned the equally un-American lesson of submission. For the South had undergone an experience that it could share with no other part of America—though it is shared by nearly all the peoples of Europe and Asia—the experience of military defeat, occupation, and reconstruction.

Nothing about this history was conducive to the theory that the South was the darling of divine providence.

2

In his book, *The Irony of American History,* Reinhold Niebuhr conducts an astute analysis of national character and destiny that emphasizes another set of American pretensions, which he calls the illusions of innocence and virtue. These illusions have their origins in both North and South, though at a period before there was any distinct regional consciousness. They were fostered by the two great moral traditions of early national life, New England Calvinism and Virginia deism of the Jeffersonian school. While they differed upon theology, theocrats and deists were agreed that their country was "God's American Israel," called out of a wicked and corrupt Old World and set apart by Providence to create a new humanity and restore man's lost innocence. I believe that Niebuhr would agree that what I have described as the American legend of success and victory has assisted in fostering and perpetuating these illusions of innocence and virtue. At any rate he demonstrates that these illusions have been preserved past infancy and into national adulthood. Arriving at man's estate, we have suddenly found ourselves in possession of immense and undreamed of power and compelled to use this power in ways that are not innocent and that cover us with guilt. In clinging to our infant illusions of innocence along with our new power, writes the theologian, we are "involved in ironic perils which compound the experiences of Babylon and Israel"—the perils of overweening power and overweening virtue.

Our opposite numbers in the world crisis, the Russian Communists, are bred on illusions of innocence and virtue that parallel our own with ironic fidelity, even though they are of very different origin and have been used to disguise (perhaps even from themselves) what seems to us much greater guilt of oppression and cruelty. They combine these illusions with Messianic passions that find a paler reflection in one layer of American conscience. Looking upon their own nation as the embodiment of innocence and justice, the Russians take it for granted that America is the symbol of the worst form of capitalistic injustice. Both America and Russia find it almost impossible to believe that anyone could think ill of them and are persuaded that only malice could prompt suspicions of motives so obviously virtuous. Each tends to regard the other as the only force wilfully thwarting its dream of bringing happiness to all mankind.

There are many perils, both for our nation and for the world, inherent in this situation—and they do not all come from abroad. We are exasperated by the ironic incongruities of our position. Having more power than ever before, America ironically enjoys less security than in the days of her weakness. Convinced of her virtue, she finds that even her allies accuse her of domestic vices invented by her enemies. The liberated prove ungrateful for their liberation, the reconstructed for their reconstruction, and the late colonial peoples vent their resentment upon our

nation—the most innocent, we believe, of the imperial
powers. Driven by these provocations and frustrations,
there is the danger that America may be tempted to exert
all the terrible power she possesses to compel history to
conform to her own illusions. The extreme, but by no
means the only expression, would be the so-called pre-
ventive war. This would be to commit the worst heresy
of the Marxists, with whom it is dogma that they can
compel history to conform to the pattern of their dreams
by the ruthless use of force.

To save ourselves from these moral perils, Dr. Niebuhr
adjures us to disavow the pretensions and illusions of innocence derived from our national childhood, along with
all self-righteousness, complacency, and humorless idealism. If we would understand our plight and prepare for
the role we must play, we must grasp the ironic implications of our history. I realize that Niebuhr's view of human
strivings is based on theology, a subject definitely beyond
my province. Whatever its theological implications and
I have frankly never explored them—the view has a validity apart from them that appeals to the historian. Yet the
ironic interpretation of history is rare and difficult. In the
nature of things the participants in an ironic situation are
rarely conscious of the irony, else they would not become
its victims. Awareness must ordinarily be contributed by
an observer, a nonparticipant, and the observer must have
an unusual combination of detachment and sympathy. He
must be able to appreciate both elements in the incongruity
that go to make up the ironic situation, both the virtue and
the vice to which pretensions of virtue lead. He must not

be so hostile as to deny the element of virtue or strength on the one side, nor so sympathetic as to ignore the vanity and weakness to which the virtue and strength have contributed. Obviously, the qualifications of the ironic historian are pretty hard to come by.

3

Now the South is deeply involved at present in the ironic plight of our country as a full-fledged participant. In fact, the headlong precipitancy with which the South has responded to the slogans of nationalism in recent world crises has often exceeded that of other sections of the country. Mass response sometimes suggests the zeal of recent converts. Yet there are aspects of its history and experience that make the South an observer as well as a participant, which set it apart in certain ways from the experience of the rest of the country, and which constitute a somewhat detached point of view. From that vantage point I believe it is possible for the Southern historian, and indeed all those absorbed in the study of Southern history, to make a special contribution to the understanding of the irony of American history, as well as that of the South's history.

Ironic implications of Southern history are not concealed by any legend of success and victory nor by the romantic legend of the Lost Cause. To savor the full irony of the confident and towering ante bellum dream of a Greek Democracy for the New World one has only to recall the words of a speech that Robert Barnwell Rhett made when

South Carolina seceded. The orator was picturing the historian of A.D. 2000 writing this passage: "And extending their empire across this continent to the Pacific, and down through Mexico to the other side of the great gulf, and over the isles of the sea, they established an empire and wrought out a civilization which has never been equalled or surpassed—a civilization teeming with orators, poets, philosophers, statesmen, and historians equal to those of Greece and Rome—and presented to the world the glorious spectacle of a free, prosperous, and illustrious people." As a matter of fact, in the eyes of the true believer the coming of the Golden Age did not have to await the year 2000. It had already arrived, full blown, here and now. For as Charles Sydnor has observed, "the affirmation of Southern perfection" meant just that. Blind to evils and imperfections all around them, Southerners described what they saw as the ultimate in social perfection. "Fighting to defend their way of life," says Sydnor, "they had taken refuge in a dream world, and they insisted that others accept their castle in the sky as an accurate description of conditions in the South."

The shattering of this dream and the harsh education that followed has not made the South the home of a race of philosophers. Nor does it seem to have made Southerners any wiser than their fellow countrymen. But it has provided them with a different point of view from which they might, if they will, judge and understand their own history and American history, and from which to view the ironic plight of modern America.

The meaning of the contrast between the 1930's and

the 1940's is a case in point. This transformation took place too recently for anyone to have forgotten, though many seem to have forgotten it entirely. In the thirties and well into the following decade there occurred the most thoroughgoing inquest of self-criticism that our national economy has ever undergone—not even excepting that of the muckraking and progressive era. No corner nor aspect nor relationship of American capitalism was overlooked, and no shibboleth of free enterprise went unchallenged. The prying and probing went on at every level from the sharecroppers to holding companies and international cartels. Subpoenas brought mighty bankers and public utility empire-builders to the witness stand. Nor was this activity merely the work of the wild-eyed and the woolly-haired, nor the exclusive concern of one of the major parties. It was a popular theme of the radio, the press, the screen, the theater, and even the pulpit. Some churches took up the theme and incorporated it into their programs. Universities hummed and throbbed with it. And in 1940 the former president of a public utility holding company, then candidate for President of the United States on the Republican ticket, made the theme a part of his campaign. Some of the outpouring of criticism in the thirties and forties was misdirected, some was perhaps a bit silly. But the electorate repeatedly endorsed with large majorities the party that was the more closely identified with the movement. On the whole, the people regarded it as productive of good. It was at least indicative of a healthy and self-confident society, uninhibited by fear.

Then in the mid-forties something happened. It happened rather suddenly. The floodstream of criticism dwindled to a trickle and very nearly ceased altogether. It was as if some giant sluice gate had been firmly shut. The silence that followed was soon filled with the clamor of voices lifted in accusation, denial, or recantation. No reputation was now secure from the charges of the heresy hunters, the loyalty investigators, and the various committees on public orthodoxy and conformity. Choruses were lifted in rapturous praise of the very institutions that had been so recently the objects of attack—and the choruses were joined by many of the former critics.

Surveying this remarkable transformation, the historian of the South can hardly escape the feeling that all this has happened before—or something strongly suggestive of it: that what happened in the 1940's had its counterpart in the 1830's. The earlier development was on a smaller scale, to be sure, and there were certain other obvious discrepancies to be taken into account. The dangers inherent in any such comparison between historical epochs are numerous and forbidding, for certainly no analogy is perfect since no two eras, movements, nor events are entirely alike. To suggest that modern capitalism is comparable with slavery as a system of labor would be to indulge in the loose and irresponsible language of polemics and propaganda. With due precaution and full awareness of the risks, however, one may venture a comparison, not between the two institutions, but between the public attitudes toward them and the transformations that took place in those attitudes.

What happened in the South during the 1830's is too

familiar a story to require elaboration here. Before it happened, however, we know that the Jeffersonian tradition protected and fostered a vigorous school of antislavery thought in the South. The great Virginians of the Revolutionary generation, nearly all of whom were on record for emancipation, lent their prestige to the movement. Critics of slavery spared no aspect of the Peculiar Institution. They spoke against the effect on the master as well as on the slave; they exposed the harm done the manners and morals of the South as well as its economy and society. Nor were critics mere misfits and radicals. They included men of influence and standing—politicians, editors, professors, and clergymen. Antislavery thought appeared in respectable newspapers and infiltrated evangelical sects of the Upper South particularly. In the 1820's the slave states contained a great many more antislavery societies than the free states and furnished leadership for the movement in the country. It would be false to suggest that slavery was on the way out, or, in spite of some amelioration, that the reformers made any very substantial alterations. But it is not too much to say that this was a society unafraid of facing its own evils. The movement reached a brilliant climax in the free and full debates over emancipation in the Virginia legislature during the session of 1831–1832. The effort to abolish slavery failed there as elsewhere. But as Joseph Roberts writes, "The institution was denounced as never before; it was condemned wholesale fashion by legal representatives of a slave-holding people. The vigor and breadth of the assault provide the debate with its most obvious distinction."

In spite of the vigor of the movement and the depth of its root in Southern tradition, it withered away to almost nothing in a very brief period during the middle thirties. By 1837 there was not one antislavery society remaining in the whole South. Of the thousands of voices that had been raised in outspoken protest a short while before there were to be heard only a few whispers. Opponents changed their opinions or held their tongues. Loyalty to the South came to be defined in terms of conformity of thought regarding one of its institutions. Past records and associates were scrutinized closely, and the recency with which one had denounced Northern abolitionism became a matter of public concern. The South concentrated its energies upon the repression of heresy and raised intellectual barricades against the ideas of a critical and unfriendly world. The institution that had so recently been blamed for a multitude of the region's ills was now pictured as the secret of its superiority and the reason for its fancied perfection.

4

Causes behind the transformation of attitudes in the South were numerous and complex. So are the reasons behind the transformation that has taken place in the attitudes of contemporary America. Broadly speaking, however, both of these revolutions in public attitudes were reactions to contests for power in which the two societies found themselves involved. These great struggles included many clashes of interest and issues quite apart from those concerning morals and contrasting labor systems. Even in the absence of ideological differences the strains of conflict would have been severe in each case. In the 1850's as in the 1950's, however, the crisis tended to be increasingly dramatized as a clash between different systems of labor—as slave labor versus free labor. In both the nineteenth-century war of words and the twentieth-century cold war each party to the conflict, of course, contended that the other practiced the more immoral, wicked, and shameless type of exploitation and that its own system was benevolent, idealistic, and sound. Our own opinions as to which of the parties in each crisis was the more deluded or disingenuous in its contentions are likely to be pretty firmly fixed already, and the problem is such that it need not detain us.

The point is that there exists, in spite of obvious differences, a disquieting suggestion of similarity between the two crises and the pattern of their development. The mistakes of the South, some of which have already been suggested, are readily apparent and their meaning open to all who would read and understand. In the first place the South permitted the opposition to define the issue, and naturally the issue was not defined to the South's advantage. In the second place the South assumed the moral burden of proof. Because the attack centered upon slavery, the defense rallied around that point. As the clamor increased and the emotional pitch of the dispute intensified, the South heedlessly allowed its whole cause, its way of life, its traditional values, and its valid claims in numerous nonmoral disputes with the North to be identified with one institution—and that an institution of which the South itself had furnished some of the most intelligent critics. It was a system known to have reached the natural limits of its expansion in this country already and one which was far gone on its way to abandonment abroad. Yet, in its quest for friends and allies, the South made the mistake of competing with the North for the favor of the West by insisting upon the acceptance of a system totally unadapted to the conditions and needs of the territories and often offensive to their moral sensibilities. And in looking to Europe for support from England and France, powers that might reasonably have been expected to be drawn to its cause for reasons of self-interest, the South encountered difficulties from the start. Some, though certainly not all, of these difficulties were due to the fact that those countries had already repudiated the system upon which the South had elected to stand or fall.

The knowledge that it was rapidly being isolated in the world community as the last champion of an outmoded system under concerted moral attack contributed to the South's feeling of insecurity and its conviction that it was being encircled and menaced from all sides. In place of its old eagerness for new ideas and its out-going communicativeness the South developed a suspicious inhospitality toward the new and the foreign, a tendency to withdraw from what it felt to be a critical world. Because it identified the internal security of the whole society with the security of its labor system, it refused to permit criticism of that system. To guarantee conformity of thought it abandoned its tradition of tolerance and resorted to repression of dissent within its borders and to forceful exclusion of criticism from outside. And finally it set about to celebrate, glorify, and render all but sacrosanct with praise the very institution that was under attack and that was responsible for the isolation and insecurity of the South.

Modern America is more fortunate than the ante bellum South in having an economic system which, though threatened with abandonment by other countries, has shown few of the serious weaknesses and is covered with little of the moral obloquy from which slavery suffered. And in spite of verbal orthodoxy regarding the doctrine of capitalistic free enterprise, the American political genius has shown willingness to experiment extensively with heterodox cures for ills of the orthodox system. This experimentation has, of course, been accompanied by loud protests of loyalty to the true faith. Again, modern America is not inherently nor necessarily handicapped in the struggle against its powerful antagonist by all the weaknesses that helped to doom the South to defeat.

There is, however, no cause for complacency in this good fortune. Nor does it rule out entirely the analogy that is here suggested. We should not deceive ourselves about the opinions of other peoples. While we see ourselves as morally sound and regard our good fortune as the natural and just reward of our soundness, these views are not shared by large numbers of people in many parts of the world.

They look on our great wealth not as the reward of our virtue but as proof of our wickedness, as evidence of the ruthless exploitation, not only of our own working people but of themselves. For great masses of people who live in abject poverty and know nothing firsthand of our system or of industrialism of any kind are easily persuaded that their misery is due to capitalist exploitation rather than to the shortcomings of their own economies. Hundreds of millions of these people are taught to believe that we are as arrogant, brutal, immoral, ruthless, and wicked as ever the South was pictured in an earlier war of words. Among their leaders are extremists ready with the conclusion that people so wicked do not deserve to live and that any means whatever used to destroy their system is justified by the end. One of these means is the subversive indoctrination of our labor force for insurrection. The malevolent caricature of our society contrasts so glaringly with what we believe to be the demonstrable facts—not to mention the contrast with our traditional illusions of virtue and innocence—that we are driven to indignation. And when we hear faint echoes of the same propaganda from our own allies, who no longer share our dedication to capitalism, our indignation turns into a sense of outrage.

Fortunately modern America has not yet followed the course of the South between 1830 and 1860, but the pattern of response evoked by these exasperations is not a wholly unfamiliar one. There are some unhappy similarities. Threatened with isolation as the last important defender of an economic system that has been abandoned or rejected without a trial by most of the world and that is under constant moral attack from several quarters, we have rallied to the point of attack. We have showed a tendency to allow our whole cause, our traditional values, and our way of life to be identified with one economic institution. Some of us have also tended to identify the security of the country with the security of that institution. We have swiftly turned from a mood of criticism to one of glorifying the institution as the secret of our superiority. We have showed a strong disposition to suppress criticism and repel outside ideas. We have been tempted to define loyalty as conformity of thought, and to run grave risk of moral and intellectual stultification.

Opposing each of these dangerous tendencies there is still healthy and wholesome resistance struggling to reassert our ancient tradition of tolerance and free criticism, to maintain balance and a sense of humor, to repel the temptation of self-righteousness and complacency, and to reject the fallacy that the whole American cause and tradition must stand or fall with one economic dogma. But it is too early to say that on any one of these points the healthy resistance is certain of triumph. In fact the fight is uphill, and in many instances the issue is doubtful. I am not contending that successful resistance to all the tendencies I have deplored will guarantee peace and solve the problems that plagued the 1950's, any more than I am sure that the same course would have resulted as happily in the 1850's. But I believe I am safe in contending that, in view of the South's experience, each of these tendencies should be the subject of gravest concern.

5

In the field of diplomacy and foreign relations modern America suffers from a divided mind, torn between one policy that is reminiscent of the way of the South and another more suggestive of the way of the North in the Civil War crisis. On the one hand are those who would meet the foreign challenge by withdrawing from a critical community of nations teeming with heresies and, by erecting an impregnable barricade, forcibly keep out all alien ways, influences, and ideas. Another modern group that has a counterpart in at least one school of Southerners in the 1850's are those who in the 1960's, heedless of world opinion, would brook no opposition, would not co-operate with, nor consult, other people's views, but insist that America must be strong enough to carry her way by economic coercion or by force. Suggestive also of the Southern way are those who, in competing with our opponents for the favor of uncommitted peoples, would urge upon them institutions and abstract ideas of our own that have little or no relevance to their real needs and circumstances. There are those who resent as evidence of disloyalty any defection on the part of our allies from the particular economic faith upon which we have decided to take our stand.

More reminiscent of the way of the North, on the other hand, are those who hold that this is an irrepressible conflict, that a world divided against itself cannot stand, that the issue is essentially a moral one, that we are morally obliged to liberate the enslaved peoples of the earth, punish the wicked oppressors, and convert the liberated peoples to our way of thought. The true American mission, according to those who support this view, is a moral crusade on a world-wide scale. Such people are likely to concede no validity whatever and grant no hearing to the opposing point of view, and to appeal to a higher law to justify bloody and revolting means in the name of a noble end. For what end could be nobler, they ask, than the liberation of man? Fortunately wiser counsel has generally prevailed, counsel which has charted a course of foreign policy between the perilous extremes of isolationism and world crusade. But each of the extreme courses still has powerful advocates, and neither can yet be regarded as a dead issue.

We have been admonished lately to heed the ironic consequences of the characteristic American approach to international affairs since the beginning of the present century. The main deficiencies of our policy of the last fifty years, we are told, are our legalistic and moralistic approaches to foreign relations. It is possible and even desirable, I believe, to accept the validity of this critical insight without embracing the strictly amoral, pragmatic, power-conscious policy of national self-interest that has been proposed as an alternative by those who criticize the moralistic approach. It is all too apparent that the association of the legalistic with the moralistic concept results in a torrent of indignation and bitterness against the lawbreaker and a blinding conviction of moral superiority to the enemy. Expressed in military policy and war aims these passions overwhelm reason and find no bounds short of complete submission, unconditional surrender, and total domination of the defeated people. The irony of the moralistic approach, when exploited by nationalism, is that the high motive to end injustice and immorality actually results in making war more amoral and horrible than ever and in shattering the foundations of the political and moral order upon which peace has to be built.

There would appear to be valid grounds for seeking the origins of our moralistic aberrations in the period of the Civil War. While both sides to that dispute indulged in legalistic as well as moralistic pretensions, it was the South that was predominantly legalistic and the North that was overwhelmingly moralistic in its approach. Although Southern historians have made important contributions to the understanding of that crisis, it is doubtful whether anyone has stated more aptly the ironic consequence of the moralistic approach than a Northern historian. "Yankees went to war," writes Kenneth Stampp, "animated by the highest ideals of the nineteenth-century middle classes. . . . But what the Yankees achieved—for their generation at least—was a triumph not of middle-class ideals but of middle-class vices. The most striking products of their crusade were the shoddy aristocracy of the North and the ragged children of the South. Among the masses of Americans there were no victors, only the vanquished."

Ironic contrasts between noble purposes and sordid results, between idealistic aims and pragmatic consequences, are characteristic of reconstruction periods as well as war crises. This is nowhere more readily apparent than in the postwar period through which we have recently lived and with the problems of which we are still struggling. It is especially in such times that moralistic approaches and high-minded war aims come home to roost. As usual, it is only after the zeal of wartime idealism has spent itself that the opportunity is gained for realizing the ideals for which the war has been fought. When the idealistic aims are then found to be in conflict with selfish and pragmatic ends, it is the ideals that are likely to be sacrificed. The probability of moral confusion in reconstruction policy is increased when a nation finds itself called on to gird for a new world moral crusade before the reconstruction consequent upon the last is fairly launched. Opportunities for moral confusion are still further multiplied when the new crusade promises to be fought in alliance with the public enemies of the previous moral crusade and when the new enemy happens to have been an ally in the previous crusade.

Americans have in common the memories of an earlier experiment with reconstruction and are generally conscious of some of the shortcomings of that effort. But again, the South experienced that same historic episode from a somewhat different point of view. Once Southern historians have purged their minds of rancor and awakened out of a narrow parochialism they should be in a singularly strategic position to teach their fellow countrymen something of the pitfalls of radical reconstruction: of the disfranchisement of old ruling classes and the indoctrination of liberated peoples, of the occupation of conquered territory and the eradication of racial dogma, of the problems of reunion and the hazards of reaction. They should at least have a special awareness of the ironic incongruities between moral purpose and pragmatic result, of the way in which laudable aims of idealists can be perverted to sordid purposes, and of the readiness with which high-minded ideals can be forgotten.

With all her terrible power and new responsibilities, combined with her illusions of innocence and her legends of immunity from frustration and defeat, America stands in greater need than she ever did of understanding her own history. Our European friends, appalled by the impetuosity and naïveté of some of our deeds and assumptions, have attributed our lack of historical sophistication to our lack of a history—in their sense of the word. America's apparent immunity to the tragic and ironic aspects of man's fate— that charmed and fabled immunity that once made America the Utopia of both the common men and the philoso phers of Europe—has come to be pictured as Europe's curse. For the fear that haunts Europeans is the fear that America's lack of a common basis of experience and suffering will blind her to the true nature of their dilemmas and end by plunging them into catastrophe. But the Europeans are not entirely right. America has a history. It is only that the tragic aspects and the ironic implications of that history have been obscured by the national legend of success and victory and by the perpetuation of infant illusions of innocence and virtue.

America has had cynical disparagement of her ideals

from foreign, unfriendly, or hostile critics. But she desperately needs criticism from historians of her own who can penetrate the legend without destroying the ideal, who can dispel the illusion of pretended virtue without denying the genuine virtues. Such historians must have learned that virtue has never been defined by national or regional boundaries, and that morality and rectitude are not the monopolies of factions or parties. They must reveal the fallacy of a diplomacy based on moral bigotry, as well as the fallacy of one that relies on economic coercion through the fancied indispensability of favored products. Their studies would show the futility of erecting intellectual barricades against unpopular ideas, of employing censorship and repression against social criticism, and of imposing the ideas of the conqueror upon defeated peoples by force of arms. Such historians would teach that economic systems, whatever their age, their respectability, or their apparent stability, are transitory and that any nation which elects to stand or fall upon one ephemeral institution has already determined its fate. The history they write would also constitute a warning that an overwhelming conviction in the righteousness of a cause is no guarantee of its ultimate triumph, and that the policy which takes into account the possibility of defeat is more realistic than one that assumes the inevitability of victory.

Such historians must have a rare combination of detachment and sympathy, and they must have established some measure of immunity from the fevers and prejudices of their own times, particularly those bred of nationalism, with all its myths and pretensions, and those born of hysteria that closes the mind to new ideas of all kinds. America might find such historians anywhere within her borders, North as well as South. But surely some of them might reasonably be expected to arise from that region where it is a matter of common knowledge that history has happened to their people in their part of the world.

10

A Second Look at
the Theme of Irony

THIS IS REALLY AN EXTENDED FOOTNOTE TO THE PRECEDING
essay, written to relate its ideas to more recent events.
When that essay was written in 1952 it was still possible
to say that the American legend of invincibility had been
"supported by an unbroken succession of victorious wars"
or what Americans had been taught to think of as victories,
and that the country had not so far sustained "so much as
one South African fiasco such as England encountered in
the heyday of her power." America had just recently returned from a triumphant crusade she deemed morally
impeccable. Her unique record of military triumphs was
matched by unparalleled successes in the fields of
diplomacy, domestic politics, and economic growth that
stretched back to the age of settlement. The tradition of
success and victory had been put to recent test by a generation beset by unrelenting crises, from the Great Depression that began in 1929, on through the worst of world
wars, and then without respite into the rigors of the Cold
War and a nasty little war in Korea. None of these har-
rowing experiences, nor the national response to them,

seriously called in question the national legend of success and invincibility, the assumption that in the end the American will would prevail, nor what Professor Arthur M. Schlesinger, Sr., once approvingly called "the profound conviction that nothing in the world is beyond its power to accomplish."

It was this pattern of myth sustained by experience that provoked the grave apprehensions voiced in the previous essay, the fear of risk and danger involved, both to America and to the world, in pursuing national policies grounded on the legends of success and invincibility. The risks and dangers seemed enhanced rather than diminished when those legends were combined with illusions of innocence and virtue dating from the childhood of the nation, and when the people who clung to such illusions and legends were endowed with unprecedented power and unequaled wealth. This fateful combination of myth and experience seemed to me to expose Americans to the temptation of believing that they were somehow immune from the forces of history, that "history was something unpleasant that happens to other people," and that it lay within their power to compel history to conform to the pattern of their dreams and illusions.

In the sixteen years since these reflections first took form, history has begun to catch up with Americans. The fabled immunity from frustration and defeat has faltered in its magic on several fronts, foreign as well as domestic. National security, traditionally perceived as free, a natural right of Americans, has been stripped away by revolutions in weaponry. Such security as remains, far from free, is purchased at frightful cost. With more power than ever before, more than any nation has ever had, we enjoy less security than we did in the era of national weakness. And we have found that all our power and fabulous weaponry can be ineffective in a war with a weak and undeveloped nation torn by a civil war of its own. In the meantime the innocence and virtue with which we assumed American motives are natively endowed, especially in relations with other nations, had become a stock subject of jeers and ridicule even among our friends and allies. Not only were we threatened with failure and defeat in a commitment of national honor, but we were convicted of guilt and perfidy in the court of world opinion.

Historic developments on two fronts have been mainly responsible for the rude challenge to the national legends of success and victory and the mythic corollaries of innocence and virtue. On the foreign front it was the war in Vietnam, and on the domestic front the revolt of the Negroes in the city. American involvement in problems of both types and in these very problems is not new. But heretofore it was possible and plausible to shift the burden of any failures and defeats, as well as any burden of guilt involved, to other shoulders. In the instance of Vietnam and similar fiascoes, responsibility was readily thrust upon the French or British or other "imperialist" powers. As for the problems of the Negro, they were regarded as very old and the failures, frustrations, and guilt incurred were traditionally considered the responsibilities and misfortunes of the white South. Such promptings of guilt as disturbed the American conscience over these problems were conveniently discharged in moralistic condemnations of the European imperialists or the Southern racists. Both scapegoats were readily available.

The American disposition to seek European and Southern scapegoats has not entirely disappeared. But conviction has drained out of those solutions and they are by no means so available as they once were. For whatever the origins and history of these problems, both have now come home to roost in America's front yard. Even if European imperialists pioneered the Vietnam intervention, there could no longer be any doubt that it was now an American war and that the responsibility *and* the guilt were our own. And even if the South was long the scene of the Negro's plight and Southerners bore the major part of the guilt, that situation has also changed drastically in recent years—with regard to both the scene *and* the guilt.

Recognition and acknowledgment of these momentous changes have not been wanting among Americans. American responsibility in Vietnam has been acknowledged more or less candidly by both advocates and opponents of the war policy. And the national character of the problem of Negroes and cities and national responsibility for solutions have not been generally disavowed. What is more, there has been a disposition in a few quarters to admit that America has at last encountered problems that are difficult to reconcile with traditional myths of indomitable optimism—invincibility, success, innocence, and the rest. Even in official circles there was recognition of the possibility of a resolution of the war short of anything that might be called "victory" in the traditional sense, and among the opposition there has been talk that goes much further than that. Senator J. William Fulbright, who harbors a keen awareness of the incongruity between national myth and national policies, has observed that "a nation whose modern history has been an almost uninterrupted chronicle of success . . . should be so sure of its own power as to be capable of magnanimity." And George Kennan has remarked that "there is more respect to be won in the opinion of the world by a resolute and courageous liquidation of unsound positions than in the most stubborn pursuit of extravagant or unpromising objectives." With regard to the domestic front, so representative an American as Walter Lippmann has said that "the problems of poverty and the race problem . . . are not in themselves solvable within the visible future."

The men I have quoted are thoroughly American, but to the ears of anyone attuned to the traditional rhetoric of American myth, their words will set up an immediate dissonance. One might, were it not for the derogatory connotations that cling to the word, call their pronouncements "un-American." For anyone who seriously entertains a solution for a war other than "victory," or who admits that a grave domestic problem simply has no visible solution, is clearly out of tune with the chorus of the American Way. He is marching to another drum. It may be the drum of the future (and I rather suspect that it is) but not that of the past—of tradition. In the American past, and in the predominant mind of the present as well, all wars end in victory and all problems have solutions. Both victory and solution might require some patience—but not very much. The idea of admitting defeat and the prospect of living patiently with an unsolved social problem are, to borrow Senator Fulbright's expression, "unthinkable thoughts" for most Americans.

The characteristic American adjustment to the current foreign and domestic enigmas that confound our national myths has not been to abandon the myths but to reaffirm them. Solutions are sought along traditional lines. A vast amount of impatience over current policies is evident in many quarters, but it is chiefly impatience with fulfillment of traditional American myth based on unshaken expectation of fulfillment. Critics and advocates differ over which among the sometimes irreconcilable components of national mythology they most cherish. Generally speaking, the advocates of current policy cling to victory and success as the indispensable goals, while the critics cherish above all the legend of innocence and virtue. Some proponents of current policy will insist that their measures will insure the triumph of both victory and virtue, success as well as innocence. And a few of the opposition will make equally comprehensive claims for their own position. Whatever the differences and enmities that divide advocates and opponents (and they are admittedly formidable), both sides seem predominantly unshaken in their adherence to one or another or all of the common national myths. This is not true of some of the critics. For example, it does not apply to the three prominent critics quoted above. But I do not believe their position is typical or characteristic of the opposition generally expressed.

In behalf of the prevailing policy of massive intervention in Vietnam, defenders have from time to time announced numerous objectives by way of justification and defense. These have been described as sacred "commitments." Foremost among them was the commitment to the freedom of the South Vietnamese, their right to determine their own destiny free from outside coercion. But as the years passed and the Vietnamese will to freedom became less conspicuous than American coercion of the Vietnamese, the suspicion grew that we had a deeper commitment to American pride than to Vietnamese freedom. According to the legend of invincibility, American will must prevail in the end. That an exception should be made for a war with rag-tag guerrillas of a small and heretofore unheard-of undeveloped country of Southeast Asia was all the more unthinkable. How could the most powerful country in the world at the peak of its power, with an unbroken history of supposedly victorious wars, submit to such humiliation? What President could accept the disgrace of being the first to lead his country to defeat? What American electorate would rally to his support if he did?

The legend of national innocence as well as that of invincibility figured largely in the preoccupations of those who sought to justify the war and defend American policies. They disavowed the guilt associated with "imperialism." Unlike European powers that preceded them in this area, America had no "imperialistic" motives. We sought no territorial aggrandizement, coveted no "colony," desired no subject people. We came to liberate, not to enslave. Our purpose was to assure self-determination and freedom. And above and beyond that, we pledged post-war reconstruction with munificent subsidies for development, industrialization, and modernization. We called it "welfare imperialism," if we used the latter word at all. Granted these policies served our national interests, they served equally the interests of freedom, democracy, and peace the world over. It was for these larger ends that we were lavishly spending blood and treasure. Once the war was over, we promised prompt and complete withdrawal of our enormous forces—within six months, we said. Thus we demonstrated our guiltlessness and proclaimed our innocence. Our real motives were benevolent and altruistic, we protested, and we showed clean hands to a skeptical world.

Opponents of national policy had many complaints and a variety of alternatives to propose. Broadly speaking, however, they were divided between those primarily concerned with defeat and victory and those chiefly preoccupied with guilt and innocence. For convenience we shall refer to the two as Right-wing and Left-wing opposition. Granted that many opponents were concerned over fear of both defeat and guilt and that a great many ranged between extreme Right and extreme Left, we shall try to clarify issues by examining the two extremes.

On the extreme Right were those so appalled by the suggestions of any solution short of total victory as to oppose rigidly any sort of compromise, concession, even negotiation. To them such approaches to war smacked of weakness and defeat and were unworthy of our tradition. For the same reasons they distrusted the inhibitions of limited-war policy, along with all the self-imposed restrictions on targets, weapons, manpower, and areas of operation. Their philosophy held that the purpose of war is victory, and that all means to that end are justified. The only valid limitations on the doctrine of hot pursuit should be capture and surrender. To them a "no-win war" was abhorrent. If the price of victory be the risk of precipitating war with mightier powers, that must be accepted. If escalation in weaponry be an inevitable consequence, then it had best come while our own arsenal of "unconventional" weapons was the largest. If that meant a nuclear showdown in the end, we were better prepared for that now than we might be later on.

The extreme Left was occupied by those to whom the present reality of guilt was far more intolerable than the prospect of defeat, either partial or total. Their dedication to the ideal of national innocence so far exceeded their commitment to the myth of invincibility as virtually to exclude all concern with the goal of victory. They dismissed the official disavowals of "imperialistic" motives with contempt. They branded promises of freedom, self-determination, democracy, and postwar development as outrageous hypocrisy. And they scornfully contrasted our pretensions of benevolence and altruism with realities of civilian casualties, scorched earth, chemical warfare, burned babies, and a devastated and demoralized country.

So tormented were those of the Left by the grotesque incongruity between their cherished self-image of national innocence and the realities of national guilt that they were driven to believe that any means whatever were justified by the end of restoring lost innocence or at least stopping the increment of intolerable guilt. Some would go so far as to carry protest to the point of disruptive tactics and disruption to the point of paralyzing their own government. Some would not only renounce any co-operation with our military forces in this war but would renounce resort to force and military means in any circumstances. They would not only renounce our foreign commitments in the present crisis but would renounce all future commitments and responsibilities, especially in Asia, if they imply force. They would, in effect, leave the shaping of foreign affairs to those powers unencumbered with legends of national innocence and accustomed to incurring guilt in the exercise of power and the pursuit of policy.

In the domestic crisis over Negro Americans and the cities, opinion was not so schematically divided by dedication to one or another of the national myths as in the foreign crisis. While there was more ambivalence, however, both the legend of success and that of innocence were powerfully coercive in shaping attitudes and expectations. With regard to the Negro the nation lacked even so much substance in its history to support a myth of success and innocence as it enjoyed in regard to war and foreign policy. The one great failure in national history was Reconstruction, and that was the failure to solve the problem of the Negro's place in American life. So strange

and unprecedented, so incongruous with national tradition and experience was this raw encounter with failure
and frustration, that the response was a refusal to acknowledge it or face up to its consequences. Many even
refused to admit that it was a failure. Others brushed
over the question by stress on the virtue displayed and
the innocence earned in freeing the slaves. Had they not
fought a most terrible and bloody war for that purpose?
Had they not saved the Union and abolished slavery?
Had they not then written into the Constitution guaran-
tees of citizenship, franchise, civil rights, justice, and equality before the law for Negroes? And did not all these
good works add up to a "Treasury of Virtue" on which
not only the Civil War generation might draw, but their
posterity for generations to come?

To be sure, many of the promises went unfulfilled or
forgotten and injustice, discrimination, and brutality went
unpunished. A terrible burden of guilt was incurred in
all this, but the guilt was conveniently regionalized. The
freedmen and the great majority of their descendants continued to live in the South for three generations. The
South was historically saddled with the war guilt already.
It was traditionally considered the source of all the old
troubles, and it came natural to think of the region as
the cause of all subsequent racial troubles as well. The
South was the theater of the Negro's sufferings and be-
trayals, and the South therefore bore the responsibility
and the guilt. Whatever measures the nation took to correct these evils—and they were few and far between—
were aimed at the supposed seat of the trouble, the South.

After nearly a century of waiting, the Negroes themselves took the lead of a great movement in their own behalf. Since the more prominent leaders of the movement were Southern, since the main theater of operation was initially in the South, and since it was called a "civil rights" movement, the whole thing carried powerful and instant appeal to the North. All of the elements appeared to fall into grooves of thought and expectation traditionally associated with an historic problem. Once more the South was mobilized to frustrate fulfillment of racial justice. Once more the demands of the black people were essentially the right to vote, to equality before the law, and to equal and unsegregated access to schools and other opportunities. These elemental rights were generally assumed to be assured them outside the South already. Here at last was the time and opportunity to settle old scores in the South.

With an outpouring of moral and missionary fervor unequaled in the cause of the Negro since the First Reconstruction, the North mobilized for another crusade. Cavalcades of freedom riders, cadres of organizers, agitators, and preachers, task forces of teachers, lawyers, and psychiatrists, and shock troops of SNCC and CORE sped southward. Money from government, foundations, labor organizations, and private pockets poured after them. Congress responded with a first, a second, a third, and a fourth civil rights act and followed up with appropriations and priorities for enforcement. Two Presidents threw all the weight of their office and personal prestige onto the scale. When local resistance proved defiant and intractable, airborne divisions of troops were ordered south. When organizers staged dramatic confrontations between Negro demonstrators and white resistance, thousands flew southward to take part in mass freedom marches.

Slowly but unmistakably Southern resistance gave ground before the onslaught of the crusaders. The old barriers of segregation, discrimination, and disfranchisement began to crumble. School integration began to be more than token, Negroes began to appear in trains, theaters, libraries, and hotels as well as in jobs and positions of authority from which they had long been excluded. They also began to vote in large numbers and to hold elective as well as appointive offices. Much remained to be done, but many of the crusaders began to be dazzled by their accomplishments. At long last it seemed as if the failures and frustrations of a century might be redeemed by another great success in the American tradition. And all the national guilt projected on the South might be expiated, and the tarnished image of national innocence restored to its original brightness and purity.

Then, on the apparent eve of triumph, the crusaders' dream of success and restored innocence was cruelly shattered. For suddenly over their shoulders they caught sight of their own cities on fire, literally aflame. The very people whose liberation they were about to achieve and whose eternal gratitude they assumed they had won in the South were now in open rebellion against them in the North. Even while they were engaged in their crusade below the Potomac, the scales had tipped and the majority of Negro

Americans no longer lived in the South, but for the first time in our history in the North. And in the transition alarming changes had occurred. Unlike the familiar black supplicants in the South, black rebels in the North spoke of violence instead of nonviolence, hatred instead of love. Instead of "We Shall Overcome," sung with linked arms and clasped hands, came war cries of black nationalism. And in place of pleas for integration, came rejection of whites and white society—paternalism and all.

Harder for the Northern paternalists to bear than ingratitude was the burden of imputed guilt, the very kind of guilt they had traditionally projected on the South and had just been engaged in expiating in Mississippi. Their predominant reaction was incredulity. They simply refused to believe their eyes. After three summers of ghetto riots and burning cities, more than three-fourths of the whites still believed that "Negroes are treated the same as whites" and that there was no danger of riots in their own cities. Only one in a hundred thought Negroes were treated badly. The ghetto riots were popularly attributed, as lesser troubles traditionally had been in the South, to "outside agitators" and "Negroes demanding too much." For all that, the seething black ghettoes continued to erupt in violence, more of them each summer, and some did not wait for the "riot weather." Scores of cities exploded and in the worst explosions military interventions, human casualties, and physical destruction far exceeded anything of the sort that had occurred in the South up to that time. The terrifying stories and pictures of these riots were spread before a world that enjoyed more than a normal appetite for news of American failures and frustrations and embarrassments.

The shame of failure and guilt and the painful exposure of American pretensions of success and innocence were more than some could bear. The costs to sanity and judgment were staggering. On the Right were those more unhinged by frustration than by guilt and willing, in order to evoke a semblance of success in the form of control, to restore "law and order" at any cost. They advocated harsh repression not only of violence and crime but of dissent and agitation as well. On the extreme Left were those driven to desperation by the burden of guilt. In order to expiate the guilt and restore undisputed innocence they were willing to condone or even abet the strategy of the extreme black militants to "burn down America" in the quest for justice.

Between Right and Left were growing numbers of Moderates or Liberals who sought success and innocence by redefining or abandoning traditional goals and policies to which they had long been committed. They said that while racial integration may be desirable in the South, conditions in the metropolitan North made it impracticable in the foreseeable future. Integrated schools were dangerous or impossible and so with integrated housing and society in general. They were prepared to write off the integration effort as futile for the present, at least in the metropolitan North. Instead they would adopt racial separatism—the division of society into two more or less distinct communities according to race. The goal would be peaceful coexistence for the present, with eventual in

tegration once it becomes practicable. Those familiar with
the old separate-but-equal dialectic of Southern segrega-
tionists, so recently discredited and abandoned, will hear
familiar echoes in this new trend of Northern thought.
They will also perceive in this rather disingenuous flight
from failure and guilt an unacknowledged abandonment
of principle.

The painful truth that Americans were so frantically
fleeing was that history had at last caught up with them.
It was no longer "something unpleasant that happens to
other people," for it was happening to them too in their
own part of the world. Neither their fabulous wealth nor
their unequaled power, their superb technology nor their
legendary "know-how," nor all these endowments combined assured them of success in solving their most press-
ing problems. On both the foreign front and the domestic
front they had at last encountered problems that defied
solutions of the traditional short-term sort and mocked
their religion of optimism. In redoubling their commitments and escalating their efforts at solutions, they seemed
to flounder deeper in frustration and failure and to incur
an ever mounting burden of guilt. And yet they clung
desperately to their myths of invincibility and success,
national innocence and virtue, and reasserted their hope
of compelling history to conform to the pattern of their
myths and dreams by the unstinted use of their wealth
and power.

What then of the suggestion I made sixteen years ago
that the Southern heritage, the collective experience of
the Southern people, might some day serve as a useful

counterbalance to the national experience and national myths? Revolutionary changes of the last two decades have blurred the distinctiveness of the South. In the "Great Barbecue" following the Second World War the South took a seat and helped itself to more than a taste of success and affluence and what it has learned to call "progress." It also shared in the national afflatus of victory and self-righteousness that came of the war. And somewhat against its will the South earned a small treasury of virtue in righting some of the ancient wrongs against its Negro people. These recent experiences have doubtless won more Southern adherents to the national myths, but they have not changed the region's earlier history. That history does not include an unbroken experience of invincibility, success, opulence, and innocence. The South does not share the national myths based on these experiences, not legitimately at least, and only vicariously at best. That is for the good and simple reason that, unlike the nation, the South has known defeat and failure, long periods of frustration and poverty, as well as human slavery and its long aftermath of racial injustice. Some of this heritage lies far enough back to be dimmed by time, but not all—not the poverty, the frustration, nor all of the guilt. And then quite recently the South has had to learn anew the bitter lesson history tried with only limited success to teach a century earlier—how to accommodate itself to conditions that it had repeatedly sworn it would never accept. "Never" was the South's slogan. "Never." But it did accommodate. It did eventually accept. The South's experience with history has rather more in common with the ironic and tragic experience of other nations and the general run of mankind than have other parts of America. National experience and the myths based on it have isolated Americans to the degree that they qualify in foreign eyes as the "Peculiar People" of modern times, quite as much as Southerners qualified for that dubious distinction in the last century. It is a dangerous isolation. If there were ever a time when Americans might profit from the un-American heritage of the South, it would seem to be the present.

But if history had caught up with America, it would seem that the irony of history had caught up with the ironist—or gone him one better. For in this fateful hour of opportunity history had ironically placed men of presumably authentic Southern heritage in the supreme seats of national power—a gentleman from Texas in the White House and a gentleman from Georgia in the State Department. And yet from those quarters came few challenges and little appreciable restraint to the pursuit of the national myths of invincibility and innocence. Rather there came a renewed allegiance and sustained dedication. So far as the war and the pursuit of victory were concerned, the people of the South seemed to be as uncompromising as those of any part of the country and more so than many. Perhaps it was unrealistic to expect Southerners to be any the wiser for their historical experience, even if it could be assumed that their fellow Americans have been the more misguided for theirs. Historians are more skeptical of the alleged "lessons of history" than the laity, and they should know better than anyone else that when there is a choice between the "right" lesson and the "wrong," mankind has a strong predilection for the latter.

There is also some lack of realism in expecting politicians of Southern origin and identification to embody their native heritage in national statesmanship. This is especially true when the greatest handicap the politician suffers in his struggle for national power is his regional identification and when his first and constant concern is to divest himself of as much of the regional incubus and handicap as possible. Such a politician will instinctively avoid offending national sensibilities and be especially scrupulous in his homage to national myths. If the South's un-American experience of history provides no real immunity from national myths for Southerners, it promises even less for non-Southerners.

America will have to work out the incongruities between modern realities and the myths of national childhood as a national problem. On the foreign front it is the incongruity between power and innocence. So long as we lacked power we were necessarily innocent of using it. The first real power we enjoyed was concealed by the covert form in which economic, as opposed to military, power is exerted. Once we acquired military power we vowed we would use it only in righteous and unselfish causes. When this proved illusory, we disavowed the responsibilities of power and retreated to isolation. Emerging from isolation at last, we returned to the doctrine of righteous causes and added the corollary of "welfare imperialism." Throughout we have clung to the dogma that power is compatible with innocence. We have yet to acknowledge the truth of Reinhold Niebuhr's dilemma, that "power cannot be wielded without guilt" and that "the disavowal of the responsibilities of power can involve an individual or nation in even more grievous guilt."

On the domestic front the ironic incongruity is between opulence and the myth of equality and virtue. For a long time we managed to reconcile these incompatibles superficially by assuming that our prosperity was the reward of our virtue. And in answer to complaints that the prosperity was unequally distributed we opened new frontiers or increased production so that the inequities of distribution were less obvious or more easily borne. This worked fairly well for a time. But now with production at an all-time high and ever accelerating, the inequities of distribution paradoxically increase and multiply along with the gross national product. And so do resentment and rebellion in the ghettos.

Up to a century ago the South did not worry about the inequities of distribution. Yet in those days the South sometimes thought of itself as prosperous, even opulent. Of course the Negroes shared little of the prosperity, but then nearly all of them were slaves and received nothing but bare maintenance for their labor. It was not until after the revolutionary change of emancipation—and partly because of it—that the South awoke to the illusory character of its prosperity. Gunnar Myrdal, the Swedish scholar, has recently told us that American prosperity is in large part illusory too. "The common idea that America is an immensely rich and affluent country," he writes, "is very much an exaggeration. American affluence is heavily mortgaged. America carries a tremendous burden of debt to its poor people." He reckons the cost of rehabilitating our slums and paying the enormous debt to the thirty million or more Americans, both black and white, who receive little more than bare maintenance from the prosperous economy they serve, in the trillions of dollars. The paying of that debt may well require changes as revolutionary as the Reconstruction of the South a century ago. One hopes that the coming ordeal will not take so long and that the outcome will be more satisfactory. But if so, then we know from Southern experience that the political and economic revolution will have to be accompanied by a revolution in attitudes as well and a wholesale abandonment of myths—particularly those of moral complacency and innocence and those that hold equality and justice and virtue compatible with opulence. In all this, Americans might still have something to learn, if they would, from the un-American and ironic experience of the South with history.

11

Look Away, Look Away

I ONCE QUOTED HENRIK IBSEN AS SAYING THAT THE LIFE-span of what he called a "truth" was at most twenty years and that any truth surviving that long appeared "shockingly thin." It is now four decades—twice the maximum life-span thus allotted any truth it might contain—since the essay entitled "The Irony of Southern History" was first published, in 1953. Fifteen years later I was induced to add "A Second Look at the Theme of Irony" to a revised edition of *The Burden of Southern History*. In that reassessment of 1968 I felt obliged to concede that while "history had caught up with America, it seems that irony has caught up with the ironist—or gone him one better." And now, twenty-five years later, comes an indulgent invitation to venture a third look.

The modifications or concessions made a quarter of a century ago were inspired by unforeseen developments at home and abroad. The original essay had made much of the contrast between the South's historic experience of defeat and failure and the national illusions of innocence, success, and invincibility that Reinhold Niebuhr had emphasized as components of his thesis in *The Irony of American History*. By 1968, however, it was becoming plain that all these ironic components of American character and distinctiveness—virtue and innocence as well as invincibility—had been seriously compromised if not shattered in Vietnam by the longest war the nation ever fought and the first one it acknowledged losing. Southerners were no longer the only Americans who had experienced collective failure, lost innocence, and military defeat, even though the South's defeat was somewhat closer to home and far more costly in blood and treasure and humiliation than the one in Southeast Asia. Anyway, Southerners were no longer in quite the same position to read fellow Americans lessons on illusions of innocence and hubris. And furthermore any claims made for regional distinctiveness based on an "un-American" encounter with history were somewhat embarrassed.

It is clearer to me now than it was originally that in applying Niebuhr's thesis to North-South relations my real purpose lay more in supporting belief in the continuing distinctiveness of the South than in establishing the irony of its history. That accounts for any sense of lost faith in the thesis that might have been conveyed in the reassessment of 1968. Whatever the cost to the cause of persisting distinctiveness of the South, however, the Vietnam disaster and other events of the intervening fifteen years contributed substantially to the ironies of Southern history. Not only had the strongest support for the Vietnam war come from the South, but so also had the President and the Secretary of State who led the crusade, presumably in pursuit of the national myths of innocence and invincibility and with no apparent acknowledgment of the Niebuhrean stricture that "power cannot be wielded without guilt."

Contemporaneous with the crisis in foreign affairs another occurred in domestic affairs that was even richer in proliferating ironies. This was the national resort to violence by the black people who in 150 major riots looted and put to the torch the slums of cities from one coast to the other for four summers from 1965 to 1968. Some of the ironies involved were inadequately explored in the previous reassessment. Not overlooked, to be sure, was that Northern, rather than Southern, cities were the principal sites of these yearly waves of violence and their casualties in life and property. Nor escaping comment was the incredulity of North-based crusaders for black rights in the South upon seeing their philanthropic sacrifices rewarded by flaming cities and militant threats to "burn down America." This sort of thing was deemed to be properly confined to the South.

But there are still other ironic aspects to be explored. One is the violence with which the oppressed black people chose to celebrate the triumph of the doctrine of nonviolence, for the watchword and rallying cry of the civil rights crusade had been nonviolence. Martin Luther King, Jr., had constantly invoked the example of Mahatma Gandhi, and King's Southern black followers had faithfully complied in the face of constant violence by law and by mob on the part of whites. But the triumph of the non-violent strategy, marked by the signing of the Civil Rights Act of 1964 and the Voting Rights Act of 1965, was followed immediately—

five days after the latter event—by the explosion in Los Angeles that touched off four summers of black violence. Accompanying this reversal of the black strategy and direction of march was a second about-face ordered by black-power leaders of the militant persuasion who renounced King's aim of racial integration and proclaimed an aggressive racial separatism and nationalism.

It remains to consider the implications for my thesis of the President under whose administration these contradictory racial developments took place. He was of course the same chief executive who led the Vietnam struggle to vindicate the national myths of innocence and invincibility. And Lyndon Baines Johnson was as Southern in origins, accent, personality, and political style as a politician with aspirations for national leadership could have been at mid–twentieth century. Here the ironies begin to multiply. Johnson was quite aware of the penalties and limitations his Southern identity would entail in any circumstances, but more especially given the role into which history had thrust him—to preside over and implement the Second Reconstruction.

This role brings to mind the one that history assigned the first President Johnson, another Southerner brought to the highest office by the assassination of his predecessor, and destined to preside over the First Reconstruction just one century before, in the 1860's. The contrast between the ways in which the two Presidents Johnson responded to their reconstruction assignments could hardly have been more striking. Andrew Johnson aligned himself politically with opponents of equal rights for black freedmen in the

North and with white resistance in the South, and by liberal use of pardon and veto and appointive power did all
he could to block or frustrate the enforcement of civil lib-
erties, voting rights, and equal protection of the law for the
newly created black citizens.

Lyndon Johnson a century later pursued precisely the opposite course in his reconstruction strategy. And it *was* his in
the peculiar sense that it was he and not Northern crusaders
who proposed and railroaded through Congress the Second
Reconstruction laws. These included not only the Civil
Rights Act of 1964, originating in President John F.
Kennedy's administration, and the Voting Rights Act of
1965, but by October, 1966, the passing of a grand total of
181 of the 200 measures he proposed in order to advance his
War on Poverty and Great Society programs. Most of these
measures were addressed to the health, housing, education,
safety, employment, environment, and welfare needs of the
poor, especially the black poor. It was time, he told a joint
session of Congress, that "the richest nation on earth . . .
bring the most urgent decencies to all your fellow Americans." And, he concluded, "We *shall* overcome." He could
eventually boast that "there has never been an era in
American history when so much was done for so many in
such a short time." And he could lay claim to doing more
for black people's rights than any of the other Presidents
since Lincoln and to having gone on to score more humanitarian legislation than all of them put together.

Of course it was one thing to get laws passed and another to get them implemented and enforced. It was over
those obstacles that the First Reconstruction stumbled and

eventually came a cropper—those as well as the stubborn resistance of Southern whites and the opposition or acquiescence of Northern whites. How then did the response of whites to the reconstruction efforts of the 1960's compare with their reaction to those of the 1860's? Southern whites were probably more united initially in their undeclared war against the civil rights crusade than they had been in their declared war against the Union in the Civil War. There were white Southern dissenters from both, to be sure, but the second struggle, though not nearly so bloody, lasted twice as long, from 1955 to 1965, and the reconstruction sequel to the second was not so violent as that which Claude Bowers describes in *Tragic Decade,* nor so "tragic."*

Militant white resistance to desegregation came before a new version of surrender and reconstruction. Initial reaction to the *Brown* decision of 1954 against segregated public schools was deceptively mild. But within a year signals were handed down from the upper ranks of society condoning in various ways "responsible" law defiance, signals that were interpreted in lower ranks as authorizing revivals of Ku Kluxery. That message came early from the White Citizens' Councils, which professed moderation while advocating defiance of the law. Essentially the same

---

*I have used the term "Second Reconstruction" in earlier writings more loosely than I do here, to refer to the years beginning in 1954 (the *Brown* decision) and continuing through the civil rights movement and beyond. Here I divide those years into two periods: first the period of Southern white resistance by means violent and nonviolent from 1955 to 1965, and second the years following, without a precise terminal date, in which resistance diminished, for which I reserve the term "Second Reconstruction."

message was embodied in the "Southern Manifesto" of 1956 signed by 101 out of 128 Southern Congressmen and Senators. By that time "massive resistance" had become the established doctrine in the South, and in the Lower South desegregation was regarded as a dead issue. To enforce conformity, books, newspapers, periodicals, films, radio, and television were subject to censorship, and tolerance of dissent was all but abandoned.

Violence against black people was conducted individually at first, and included murder, arson, lynching, and various acts of terror. Mass action to block school desegregation came in response to exploitation of the issue by politicians. The military phase of resistance began in 1957 when Governor Orval E. Faubus of Arkansas called out National Guardsmen to prevent nine black children from entering a high school in Little Rock. President Dwight D. Eisenhower responded by ordering in paratroops—the first intervention of Federal troops to protect black citizens since the Compromise of 1877 that ended the First Reconstruction. Military action against mob and state resistance came elsewhere, the most violent and bloody at Oxford, Mississippi, with Governor Ross Barnett in personal command, over the registration of James Meredith at the university. After the Battle of Oxford came a more farcical battle at the University of Alabama. Governor George C. Wallace, just inaugurated with the slogan Segregation Forever, went through the motions of "standing in the schoolhouse door" for the cameras before Federal troops forced integration.

A feature of the Second Reconstruction that recalls black

activism in the First was the awakening of Southern blacks in the 1960's, with youth in the lead, to take command of their own liberation. Promising whites to "wear you down by our capacity to suffer" and win by "appeal to your heart and conscience," King set the example followed by thousands of young men and women who were mobbed, beaten, attacked with dogs and fire hoses, and jailed by the thousands. Using the passive and legal protests of boycotts, sit-ins, freedom rides, and marches, black activists voiced their rhetoric in words and music of Baptist and Methodist hymns as familiar to whites as to black Protestants. And they saw the walls of segregation begin to crumble as Southern white sentiment began to shift to compliance with the law, and national sympathy became engaged in the cause.

The Deep South still remained a fortress of defiance, however, and Birmingham became the symbol of it as images of bombed and burned houses and snarling police dogs flickered across the television screens of the world. The worst atrocity was the bombing of a black church that killed four girls and resulted in the killing of two boys by the police who were dispersing protesters against the bombing. The Justice Department counted a national total of 758 racial demonstrations that followed the Birmingham outburst.

Interracial violence flamed in several Southern cities. White violence climaxed in Selma, Alabama, in March, 1965, over frustrated efforts to register black voters. To rally national support King organized a march from Selma to Montgomery in protest and encountered at the outset violence from state troopers with nightsticks and tear gas. That scene, as expected, captured national sympathy, and some twenty thousand supporters from all parts of the country responded to King's appeal to join in the final stage of the march. The march and the civil rights crusade came to a thunderous climax in Montgomery with a great speech by King before the state capitol where the Old Confederacy was born.

Montgomery in 1965 might have been called the Appomattox of the South's second embattled resistance had not George Wallace continued his resistance and carried his campaign into the North. But the first Lost Cause seems to have done something to prepare Southern whites for the second, involving the obsession with race that had suffused and coerced all aspects of regional life for a century and a half. This time the embattled laid down their arms with a sense of relief, even some gratitude, and accepted their defeat with more grace. To quote myself on this subject thirty-five years ago, "The South has been called on before to bear the brunt of a guilty national conscience. . . . One could hope that the South's experience in these matters might stand it in good stead, that having learned to swallow its own words before, it might do so again with better grace." And so it would seem to have proved. The ancient siege mentality began to melt away as the old Whites Only signs disappeared and the fortress crumbled. Whites too, in some measure, were "free at last"—at least those who wished to be—free to put the defeat and the obsession behind them, free to return to their old culture of manners, begin to extend it to black fellow citizens, and regain the respect of the world, not to mention their own self-respect.

So it was that many were ready for the Second Reconstruction, which, like the First, had begun before hostilities ended. Its author was already at work in the White House, and in 1964 President Johnson had won election on his own in a race that made civil rights a main issue. He had taken office with a personal commitment to the cause such as none of his predecessors shared. It was in the midst of the Selma crisis that he made his we-shall-overcome address to Congress. The legislation he demanded in it continued to pour out until it reached completion in 1969. Johnson had lost the South in the race he won overwhelmingly in 1964. But Southerners' compliance with his reconstruction measures probably suffered nothing for being proposed by one of their own (however "misguided") rather than by some malevolent Charles Sumner or Thad Stevens of Yankeedom.

Despite the annual slum explosions up North and the ugly episodes in the South, the relative peacefulness, for whatever reason, with which the reconstructing went forward this time is remarkable. Black voter registration soared, doubling, tripling, quadrupling in weeks. Mississippi, for example, had nearly 76 percent of its blacks registered and more black officeholders than any other state in the country by 1975. Ten years later, according to David Goldfield, five Southern states led the nation in new black officeholders, and George Wallace of Segregation Forever fame had been sworn in for his final term as Governor of Alabama with two black members in his cabinet, twenty-one in the legislature, and a larger percentage of the civil service positions filled by blacks than blacks represented in the state population. In 1975 Wallace crowned a black homecoming queen at the university to which he had sworn earlier to deny black students admission. By 1985 the largest cities of the region, as of the nation, had black mayors, and in that year Virginia installed the first man of his race ever elected Governor of a state in American history. A conservative and the grandson of a slave, Governor Douglas Wilder received 46 percent of the white vote.

As important as were these and other benefits brought about by law, accompanying them were changes made without and beyond the law, changes that for many if not most Southern black people were even more important. Not overnight, to be sure, and not without exceptions and lingering relics of the past, but with remarkable speed, the bonds of the rigid, age-hardened code of racial "etiquette" signifying white supremacy and black inferiority fell away. On the one side the shuffling Sambo of averted eyes and the old rituals of abject abasement disappeared, and on the other public use of "nigger," "boy," "auntie," and "uncle" virtually ceased and were replaced by "Mr." and "Mrs." and the elements of courtesy—not by requirement of any law but by extension of the regional code of manners to include the other Southerners. Whites had discovered in the courage displayed by blacks in individual demonstrations, mass protests, marches, and sit-ins the falsity of the old racial stereotypes and the means of liberation from the burdens of white supremacy.

To perceive and appreciate the extent of change in regional mores over the last three decades it helps to have been born, brought up, and educated in the South during the earliest decades of the twentieth century and to have returned regularly ever since for annual visits. The changes one noted over the years were registered in the places black people were to be seen and served, the new tone of assurance with which they spoke, and the ways in which whites began to address them. In spite of obstacles Southern blacks still encountered, they experienced "immeasurably more freedom, dignity, and respect" than they had in earlier years, according to Earl Black and Merle Black. Perhaps alterations of this degree and depth have occurred elsewhere in history in the relations between people of such widely disparate origins and status over so brief a period, but they do not readily come to mind.

Neglected ironies of the civil rights struggle continue to come to light. One of them is the vital role played in the movement by native white Southerners. In a forthcoming study David Chappell, a Northern historian, presents persuasive evidence that without the strong support received from Southern whites the civil rights crusade would have failed. And that support was not confined to city liberals but appeared also in small towns and communities. Chappell's most impressive evidence for this comes from testimony and correspondence files of some of the foremost black leaders of the movement in the South.

To leave the impression that all was racial harmony and peaceful compliance with the law in the South during the Second Reconstruction would be unpardonably misleading. Segregation and discrimination did not have to be enforced by law to be real. White guerrilla resistance was not confined to the backwoods, and Klan membership was on the rise in the 1970's and 1980's. However few their increased number, Klansmen and Nazis killed five in Greensboro, North Carolina, at an anti-Klan rally in 1979. The David Duke campaign of the early 1990s in Louisiana lay ahead. Lynchings and police brutality still occurred. Nearly all of this was white violence against blacks, after the unprecedented black violence of the Reconstruction years 1965–1968, the four "long hot summers" of urban riots.

The black beneficiaries of the Second Reconstruction were mainly middle-class, professional, and business people. Paradoxes and ironies abounded, however, for segregation had provided shelter for black business of the older type and black services and professionals of all types. They now fell victims to integration and the competition of superior desegregated services and institutions from which black patrons had been excluded. Nevertheless it was this class and its educated progeny who were prepared for the new freedom, jobs, opportunities, and affirmative action programs. It was they who appeared in banks, corporate offices, and in political, civil-service, white-collar, and professional positions in increasing numbers.

Not to be overlooked, either, is the dramatic if temporary improvement in the employment and economic status of black labor in the South between 1965 and 1975, especially in manufacturing. In those years the wage gap between blacks and whites dropped as blacks went from earning 38.5 percent less than whites to earning 12.6 percent less. Given the date 1965, the temptation is strong to attribute the improvement to the Civil Rights Act of that year, which prohibited racial discrimination. Undoubtedly some of the gain was attributable to the new law. But improvement began before the law was passed and coincided with a tight labor market that proved to be only temporary. The new jobs for black labor were too often in old Southern industries—textiles, tobacco, steel—that were driven by competition with cheap foreign labor to the point of closing or resorting to mechanization that left little place for labor with limited skills.

In the meantime a growing black underclass went neglected and remained largely invisible. Those remaining in the rural South sank to a desperate level of poverty, poor health, and inadequate housing. In the absence of the most elemental health care, black infant mortality was five times that of whites and black adult life expectancy ten years below white. In the cities and mill towns the plight of blacks was little if any better. Fleeing rural poverty without skills, many of them headed north. Civil rights and voting rights had done very little for this class.

The black exodus to northern cities had gained momentum in the 1940's from the pull of war industries and the push of mechanized or abandoned cotton culture. The migration slowed but continued in the 1950's and 1960's. The migrants settled into spreading ghettoes in the central-city pattern of isolation that attracted or retained few of the black professional and middle class that normally became their leaders. Whites who could afford it retreated to suburbs. When the central cities of the North exploded in the riots, lootings, and burnings of the 1960's and became notorious for their daily horrors of crime, violence, and drugs, Northern opinion underwent something of a backlash on

civil rights and affirmative action. These were remedies
thought properly intended for Southern, not Northern,
problems.

But in some measure the South had exported northward
its racial problems as it had exported its underclass. Fear
and animosity between the races outside the South exceeded that existing before the civil rights movement, and
so did violence and crime. By 1990 the South, which had
led the nation in crimes of violence for a century, having
the nine most murderous states in 1972, placed only three
of its cities in the nation's worst ten for per capita murder
and two in the worst ten for robberies. New York often led
the worst ten in the latter category and was above the big-
city average in murders. A growing percentage of these
were hate crimes, racially motivated. When Mayor David
Dinkens of New York visited South Africa in 1991 he was
told by the Nobel laureate Nadine Gordimer, "I find,
having come back and forth to America over twenty-five
years, there's more separation now between black and
white than there was some years ago. We mix more over
here." Taken aback, the mayor replied, "That's quite an
indictment."

In the meantime the exodus of black people from the
South slowed down, the tide turned, and migration in began to exceed migration out. That returning tide continued, and in the latter half of the 1980's the net black
migration into the South was 355,000 and the national
proportion of black citizens in the South reached 56 percent, after having dropped as low as 50 percent from a
twentieth-century peak of 90 percent. Interviewed about

their motives by a New York *Times* reporter in 1992, migrants returning to the South mentioned both tangibles and intangibles on the positive side. Along with better opportunities and cheaper living they mentioned friendliness, peace, a sense of safety, family roots, and the verities and familiar patterns of life. "It's like the smell of fresh washed sheets and bacon frying in the morning," said one woman. The things they were fleeing were often the opposite of those found in the South: insecurity, isolation, danger to the lives of their children and themselves, the gang and drug wars, the terrifying gunfire in the public schools.

The attractions of the South for those returning were mainly old cultural constants rather than new gains in rights and status. These were the values of place and past, the symbols and traditions of region rather than of race. They were therefore things shared with the other Southerners—the white ones. While "Southerner" still meant "white Southerner" to the racial majority, increasing numbers of blacks were acknowledging their cultural identity and laying claim to the label "Southerner" without feeling uncomfortable about it. Social scientists present graphs showing the percentage of various populations which felt "warm" toward Southerners, with the proportions of Southern whites and Southern blacks that harbored warm feelings starting in 1964 some 40 percentage points apart and converging to almost the same point above 80 percent by 1976. Non-Southern whites dropped a few points from their initial proportion of 50 percent, and non-Southern blacks rose some 30 points from about 20 percent. Black intellectuals have for years acknowledged this paradox.

The part the civil rights crusade and the Second Reconstruction played in all this and in the new order of race
relations is difficult to define, but it is hardly what it was
intended and now generally assumed to be. Some of the
results, in fact, suggest one of the classic definitions of
"irony" in the *Oxford English Dictionary:* "a contradictory
outcome of events as if in mockery of the promise and fit-
ness of things." One illustration comes from the history of
efforts to desegregate the public schools, the issue that
touched off the whole movement.

The public school issue moved desegregation into the
most sensitive zone of white fears. The white South's reaction to the Second Reconstruction effort to enforce the
Supreme Court's decision was the most stubborn and prolonged of all. It moved from ignoring to defying the law,
from renovating all-black schools, making them equal as
well as separate, to closing all public schools, and on to withdrawing into private "seg academies." Then in 1968 and the
years following came Supreme Court decisions that left little
room for evasion. Thereafter desegregation moved forward
with dispatch for a time under court-mandated supervision
and with a surprising degree of white co-operation.

In the meantime Northern and Western states, in the
grip of a backlash against black rights, were moving in-
ceasingly into separate and unequal schools in urban centers and suburbs. A study released in 1992 by the National
School Boards Association demonstrates that "the level of
total separation that had been seen as the essence of the
Southern racial system is now much more characteristic of
Illinois, Michigan, and New York than of any state in the

Deep South." Connecticut is included among states with the highest degree of segregation. Of the ten states having the largest percentages of blacks attending schools with 50 to 100 percent minority populations, only one, Texas, is Southern, with 67.9 percent, and Illinois, New York, and Michigan head the list, all in the 80 plus percent range. The study indicates that the country as a whole is moving to separate and increasingly unequal schools.

While North and West moved backward, the South moved forward through integration under court supervision and the busing of students. But desegregation too often resulted in resegregation in the cities as whites withdrew, and that in turn produced greater residential segregation than ever and resort to "neighborhood schools." White students in the public schools of Atlanta for example dropped from 50 percent to 20 percent, and blacks rose from 50 to 80 percent. A lawsuit brought by a suburban Atlanta school district and supported by the Bush administration asked for an end to court supervision of integration. A Supreme Court ruling handed down in March, 1992, could eventually end, and possibly reverse, the progress of desegregation in the metropolitan South. Finding no gain for black student achievement in desegregated schools and missing the control they once had over their own segregated schools, Southern blacks were becoming more interested in quality than in integration and nostalgic for the old black schools they controlled themselves. Some would prefer to be separate if they could be really equal in their share of state resources. In smaller towns and rural districts, however, integrated schools survived and appeared to be regarded by both races as an accepted way of life.

State colleges and universities all over the South faced dilemmas comparable with those of public schools when Federal court decisions in the second half of 1992 applied to higher education the principles of the *Brown* decision of 1954 regarding segregation in primary and secondary schools. In response Mississippi and Louisiana have proposed plans of integration that are challenged by plaintiffs before Federal district courts. The plaintiffs are black, and they are highly critical and often angry over the state integration proposals. Spokesmen for black institutions have denounced state plans as depriving them of their historic identity and mission and imposing white university standards of admission that would penalize black applicants. They would prefer equality over integration—equality in state appropriations for salaries, libraries, laboratories, and building maintenance. The ruling of the Federal district court in Louisiana was that "the dubious appeal of 'separate but equal,' whether endorsed by whites or blacks, is an anachronism that our country no longer tolerates."

The historic cotton culture, long regarded as gone with the wind, was undergoing an amazing comeback, exceeding production records when cotton was king. But this was agribusiness machine culture, not labor-intensive old-style hand culture, and it benefited few blacks. Some of what had been the richest parts of the ante bellum and post bellum cotton culture remained largely untouched or were further depleted of population by the new cotton culture.

Conspicuous among such areas were the twenty-one counties of the Alabama black belt. Deriving the name from the
rich soil and its black slaves, the black belt had been one of
the wealthiest regions of the country and its slave-holding
planter minority one of the most politically powerful elites
of the republic.

White minority dominance continued after the abolition
of slavery, but soil depletion, boll weevils, and Texas competition in the first half of the twentieth century (among
other things, to be sure) reduced what had been one of the
richest and most powerful subregions to one of its most
impoverished and politically weak. In places such as Selma, Tuskegee, Eutaw, and Haynesville the black belt became the scene of some of the most dramatic conflicts of
the civil rights movement. Perhaps the most dramatic
change resulting from the reforms has been the sudden rise
to political dominance of blacks, who had not voted or
been elected to public office since the First Reconstruction.
An outburst of activism has succeeded in electing black
candidates to fill offices monopolized by whites for a century: as judges, sheriffs, county commissioners, county
school board members, council members, city mayors.

In a study of the Alabama black belt in transition that
Allen Tullos has in progress he has unearthed some cruel
ironies. Now holding the largest percentage of elected
black officials of any regional grouping of counties in the
nation, these Alabama counties have failed to translate
political democracy into prosperity and health. The old climate of fear and intimidation has changed for the better,
but in levels of income, health, education, housing, and

industrial development, Tullos finds, these counties are now among the poorest in the whole country.

Two industrial developments are under way: one, the importation and accommodation of convicted criminals; the other the disposal of toxic wastes from other states. Greene County has under development a one-thousand-bed prison promoted by private interests which is to be financed by bonds issued by the county. The prison for profit, as large as any of Alabama's prisons, is expected to take in convicts from other states, presumably not their most tractable. One is reminded of the white Southern governments a century ago that made a business of leasing out their convicts to industrialists rather than taking them in from elsewhere. Sumter County, whose population is 70 percent black living for the most part below the poverty line but with a will to progress, has attracted the only major new industry to appear there in recent years. This is one of the largest waste dumps for toxic pesticides and chemicals, industrial sludges, and hazardous by-products in the entire nation. Other Southern counties have served as repositories for chemical weapons, especially a danger-ous nerve gas. Here is a species of irony for which the *Oxford English Dictionary* supplies no definition.

Black politicians found their rise to power in the me-tropolis as burdened with setbacks and disillusionments as did those of the countryside. Speaking from Atlanta, Michael Lomax, chairman of the Fulton County Commis-sion, said, "The irony of black political hegemony is that we gained power as cities' resources diminished and the Federal Government withdrew from the field." Louisiana can usually be depended upon for extremes of regional style in politics, as in 1991 when the black voters united with upper-class white voters against a white majority to defeat David Duke. Their slogan seen on bumper stickers was Vote for the Crook, a reference to Duke's opponent.

To wade into the field of recent revolutions in Southern politics is to risk sinking into a morass of ironies beyond my depth. It would be wiser perhaps to limit ventures into this subject to pointing out a few examples and leaving the exploring and explaining to bolder spirits. These examples are offered against a background of a Solid South for Democratic presidential candidates that lasted sixty-four years beginning in 1880 and embraced all eleven states of the Old Confederacy. One-party solidarity resulted in political impotence for the South, since neither major party was obliged to consult its needs or wishes, Democrats finding it unnecessary, Republicans useless. There followed in the 1950's and 1960's an interlude of competitive two-party politics, and then the swing to another period of virtual one-party white solidarity for Republican presidential candidates. With the exception of Jimmy Carter's victory in 1976, the Republicans carried all or almost all the South's electoral votes from 1972 through the election of 1988.

In the course of the party revolution during the Second Reconstruction the great majority of Southern whites shifted their allegiance from the white man's party of long standing to the party of Charles Sumner and Thaddeus Stevens. At the same time Southern black voters deserted the old party of Lincoln and emancipation to rally behind the old party of white supremacy. White majorities among

Southern voters in every single category of income and education, even the lowest ranks, made the South in the 1980's the most Republican of all regions, the stronghold of the party. From the region "taken for granted" so long, the states of the Old Confederacy have emerged, in the words of Earl Black and Merle Black, as "the greatest regional prize in modern presidential politics."

All three leading candidates for President in the election of 1992 laid claim to the prize by personal identification with the South in one degree or another—even the one with deeper roots in Connecticut. The winner, Governor of Arkansas for twelve years, had the strongest claim to Southern identity. And candidate Bill Clinton chose as his running mate Senator Al Gore from Tennessee, the son of a former Senator from the same state. It was the first victorious all-South ticket since 1828, when Andrew Jackson of Tennessee ran with John C. Calhoun of South Carolina. Yet Clinton and Gore won the electoral votes of only four states of the Old Confederacy—their native states plus Louisiana and Georgia—and those by narrow pluralities. All the others went to the Republican candidate, with a legal residence in Texas.

One possible reading of the 1992 election is that it signified a further decline in the importance of regional issues and identifications in presidential politics. The distinctive accent, manners, and political experience of the Democratic candidates were duly noted but appeared to be of little importance either as assets within the South or as handicaps outside. Such handicaps as Clinton suffered were personal rather than regional. All that his leading opponent could do with slurs about Clinton's much-caricatured home state proved of little or no avail. The issues to which Clinton gave priority and the changes he represented were national and generational rather than regional.

Such racial pronouncements and policies as he voiced during his campaign—and they were relatively few—sometimes appeared to have written off Southern white support and make it the more surprising that he carried the few Southern states he did. But in view of his rebuke to black racism and his opposition to racial quotas it is even more surprising that he carried 90 percent of the black vote. Clinton carried only 33 percent of the Southern white votes as against 47 percent for George Bush. His subsequent appointment of four black members to his cabinet came after the clear outbursts of pleasure among black people over his election. Among black intellectuals the demonstrations revived discussion of the old paradox of the persistent black attachment to aspects of the culture they shared so long with whites of the South.

To enter upon speculation about the prospect of President Clinton's reform program solving the problems ahead would lead us astray from the theme at hand. Even so, he at least deserves to have acknowledged the staggering difficulties he confronts. Paul Kennedy is the author of a chilling view of that prospect, *Preparing for the Twenty-First Century*, published in 1993. Writing elsewhere of "the great test facing President Clinton and his new team," Kennedy raises the question "Can any American government improve the country's chances of meeting the enormous, transitional forces for change bearing down on us?"

It is to be hoped that enough has been said by way of bringing the original theme of the 1953 essay up to date to justify this additional reassessment after forty years. How then does the theme now hold up? How much is worth salvaging? How much should be discarded? What alterations or further concessions have become necessary?

One alteration has already been made by the emphasis on the numerous Southern ironies, as compared with the Niebuhrean singular irony of American history. The theologian had foremost in mind the irony arising from the way America's enormous power and the guilt inevitably incurred by its use combine with the long-nourished myth of American innocence and virtue. I have pointed out that the South's experience did not encourage the national myths of innocence, virtue, and invincibility since it included crushing military defeat and little on which to found illusions of innocence. In so doing I was seeking in the South's marked departure from this instance of American exceptionalism the historical foundations for the region's continued distinctiveness.

Faced with the facts of America's frustration and ultimate disaster in Vietnam, I felt that in my second treatment of the theme I had to admit that the South was no longer so distinctive in its historical experience and the nation was no longer confident of either its invincibility or its innocence. I now begin to wonder if I might not have been too hasty in making this concession. History did not end with Vietnam. In the succeeding two decades American leaders did much to restore the myth. In addition to blustering interventions in tiny Central American and Caribbean republics came victory in the Gulf War and the claim of national victory in the Cold War. Of the former, President George Bush declared, "By God, we've kicked the Vietnam syndrome once and for all!" And of the latter, "By the grace of God, America has won the cold war." Two centuries earlier President Ezra Stiles of Yale described the young nation as "God's American Israel," a myth President Bush would seem to have been bent on restoring.

Even granting the survival and power of the Niebuhrean irony in characterizing American exceptionalism, however, it no longer seems as useful as it once did when applied to the irony of Southern history and its distinctiveness. I am prepared to abandon its use for this purpose for two reasons. First, while the distinctive Southern experience of defeat and failure remains fixed in history and legend more firmly than ever, it has slipped another four decades into the past and its relevance to the present is the dimmer for two more generations of Southerners. In the second place no part of the country manifested more enthusiasm for the flag-waving of the 1980's and early 1990's than the South.

One appropriate title for a revision of the old essay, entitled "The Irony of Southern History," would change the Niebuhrean singular to make it "Ironies." As indicated above, further reflection has multiplied Southern ironies that demand attention. Some of them, it is true, are shared with the North or West when they become the obverse or counterpart of Southern changes. But there are quite enough that are peculiar to the South, I believe, to characterize the region and contribute to defining its distinctiveness—perhaps even more than the means I previously used for this purpose.

We should be alert to the dangers and abuses of irony. One accepted definition, after all, is "the use of words to convey the opposite of their literal meaning." Furthermore the word "irony" is derived from a Greek word meaning "dissembler." To seek help from Sören Kierkegaard, another learned theologian and the author of *The Concept of Irony,* is not very rewarding for the purposes at hand. He tells us, for example, that "all things are possible for the ironist." But then we learn from Kierkegaard scholars that he wrote about irony ironically—and where does that leave us? The better part of wisdom would seem to be caution in all things related to this concept.

The most egregious abuse of irony would be to use it to indulge in or foster cynicism with regard to human motives and plans and their consequences. It is certainly true, as we have repeatedly seen, that in the course of the civil rights crusade and the Second Reconstruction plans often went awry and sometimes produced results the opposite of those intended. Hard-won victories in school integration could fail to produce any change in achievement for either black or white students. Desegregation produced resegregation. Much the same blurring of consequences occurred regarding voting rights and economic opportunity. Nonviolent leaders saw their followers plunged into

violence. Desegregated schools increased segregated residential housing, which in turn produced more segregated
schools. Intended beneficiaries of philanthropy could reject
the benefits offered. Do we gather from this that the movement and the effort that went into it were all for naught?
That would be a simplistic and naïve assessment of some
very complicated history.

Unintended results and undefined goals of the movement were often more important, more cherished, and
more fundamental in the changes brought about in relations between blacks and whites in the South than were
the intended and often unrealized objectives. This was not
a paper movement, not a thing of platforms, programs, demands, slogans, and points scored. The two races had lived
together in the same region for centuries. The civil rights
movement and the Second Reconstruction brought them
together in ways that no other common experience in their
history had done. Most often in the past, but not always,
they had been brought together in conflict. The arena of
conflict had been their historic meeting place. But that was
usually a meeting between superior and subordinate, op-
pressor and oppressed. The new conflict was of a different
order. It was initiated by black Southerners who fought on
the offensive, not the defensive, and with new and frustrat-
ing weapons and tactics.

White Southerners were compelled to witness black
Southerners repeatedly exposing themselves to danger in
public displays of courage, sometimes at risk of life by individuals or groups. In their culture such conduct commanded respect of a special order, *whoever* displayed it.
Year after year, back and forth, the struggle raged across

the South in sit-ins, protests, marches, and armed confrontations (blacks usually unarmed). Memorable engagements occurred at Greensboro, North Carolina; Albany, Georgia; Oxford, Mississippi; and at Selma, Montgomery, and Birmingham, Alabama. The whole struggle has found its place in the participants' common history and their regional heritage.

David Goldfield has pointed out that in recent years leaders, events, even the violence of the civil rights movement, have become "part of southern lore and iconography," cherished as part of the Southern past. Memorials and markers have been erected to identify historic moments and battles. Birmingham constructed a civil rights museum near the church where the four children were killed by bombs and has preserved the cell from which King wrote his "Letter from Birmingham Jail." The people of Memphis built a similar museum around the motel where King was assassinated. In Jackson the Mississippi State Historical Museum has added a permanent exhibit, The Struggle for Equal Rights, which includes a videotape of police violence against blacks, posters advertising black protests and Klan rallies, and printed signs of the segregation era such as White Waiting Room and Colored Entrance, unknown to the present generation but quite familiar to their parents.

Much as tourists visit Civil War battlefields, groups visit civil rights battlegrounds, sometimes to witness in the one pilgrimage as in the other bloodless reenactments of historic actions. Thus on its twentieth anniversary whites joined blacks in reenacting the Selma-to-Montgomery march, starting with the Pettus Bridge incident at Selma and end-ing with marchers being welcomed in Montgomery, by Governor George Wallace—that last scene being an alteration of history. And in Jackson at one of the annual Medgar Evers Homecoming weekends to honor the murdered black leader, former Governor Ross Barnett of Battle of Oxford fame participated in a ceremony renaming a city street in Evers' honor.

For specialists on the varieties and complexities of irony, especially those preferring its sunnier side, there is food for thought here. Perhaps Professor Goldfield has captured its essence in writing that "the greatest legacy of the civil rights movement may be its preservation of southern culture." The idea has surfaced before, anticipated in William Faulkner's *Intruder in the Dust*. It was the whites, after all, who had abandoned the large parts of their tradition they sacrificed to their long obsession with race and their fortress mentality of white supremacy. It was the blacks who got them moving from the obsessions and toward a recovery of their more genial culture.

The South has a tradition of attempting the impossible at great cost, proudly celebrating the failure, and gaining admiration for the performance. Black Southerners have made their own adaptation of the tradition in the civil rights movement. They too have gained admiration for their performance and found ample reason for savoring the ironic, if in some respects welcome, outcome. And they would seem to have added another example to that part of the region's history best understood for its numerous components of irony.

12

The Burden for
William Faulkner

IF THE COMPARISON IS NOT CARRIED TOO FAR, WILLIAM Faulkner's relation to the South resembles James Joyce's relation to Ireland. For both of them, their native culture and tradition, and to some extent their land's history, provided the subject matter of their fiction. For Joyce, that was true of all his great works; for Faulkner, fourteen of his nineteen novels, including all the great ones, center on one mythic county of his native state, and the others, but for one, on other parts of the Lower South. Both men were conscious of the provinciality of their culture and its subordinate relation to a dominant one. Both were insistent— Joyce less so—on the distinctiveness of the culture that was their own, though neither of them romanticized it. In Faulkner's case it seemed to justify the publication of a large *Glossary of Faulkner's South* with thousands of words—such as "shikepoke" and "laplink"—to assist not only his foreign readers but also non-Southerners whose native language was English.

Other comparisons, however, seem less helpful. Joyce left Ireland as a youth and remained in exile the rest of his life. Faulkner stayed rooted in Mississippi, save for stints in Hollywood to stave off bankruptcy, a few brief trips abroad, and a self-dramatized residence in Virginia toward the end. Yet both Faulkner the homebody and Joyce the exile continued to nurture powerful if contradictory emotions about "home": love and hate, devotion and dismay, loyalty and shame. Faulkner, unlike his American contemporaries—Ernest Hemingway, F. Scott Fitzgerald, Sinclair Lewis, and others of the "lost generation"—never threw off the bonds of family, clan, proliferating relatives, and community. His obstinate withdrawal into provincial Oxford, where he did nearly all his writing, could be attributed to failure, until his writings eventually made him world famous.

With the coming of fame, the mysteries and the paradoxes of the writer and his writings demanded and received more explanations, some wildly contradictory ones, while new Faulkner puzzles and enigmas kept appearing. Why, for example, was recognition so slow in coming? His greatest novels appeared between 1929 and 1936, and yet by 1945 all seventeen of his books except *Sanctuary* were out of print. Commenting on his Nobel Prize in 1950, the New York *Times* complained that his South was "too often vicious, depraved, decadent, corrupt," and added primly that "incest and rape may be common pastimes in Faulkner's 'Jefferson, Miss.' but they are not elsewhere in the United States."

The important break for Faulkner's reputation in the United States came with Malcolm Cowley's publication of *The Portable Faulkner* in 1946. Then the literary editor of

The New Republic, Cowley had already conceded that "there is no other American writer who has been so consistently misrepresented by his critics, including myself." In the introduction to his selections in 1946, Cowley spoke of Faulkner as "an epic or bardic poet in prose." And higher praise still was to come from reputable American critics. A question yet to be answered satisfactorily was why the Mississippian's accomplishment was appreciated widely abroad before it was at home. Sartre, at the peak of his anti-Americanism, declared Faulkner to be a god for French youth, and Faulkner already had a devoted public in Italy and Japan.

More and more unanswered questions piled up. How was one to reconcile the life of the writer with his achievement? A seventh-grade dropout, Faulkner was virtually without formal education, and well along in his youth without a penny or a job. A furious worker, he also became a pathological drinker, a consumer of bootleg booze in huge quantities over incredible spells, with disastrous results. Periodically confined to institutions to dry out, he eventually died in one. His wife, Estelle, shared his addiction, which was more a consequence than a cause of their unhappy and tumultuous marriage, as were her attempts at suicide. Yet they stuck it out to the end despite the long succession of his attractive young women lovers with literary ambitions, whose letters Estelle sometimes intercepted.

A family man in more than the nuclear way, Faulkner also stuck to—or was stuck with—an extended family of as many generations of relatives as happened to be around at a given time, along with proliferating nieces, nephews,

in-laws, and first, second, and third cousins once, twice, or
thrice removed. Many of them, along with "connections"
black and white, became his dependents, and he went to
any length to help them out, bail them out, or bury them
decently when he could earn, beg, or borrow the money.
This helps to explain why he was so often near bankruptcy
no matter how many Hollywood bonanzas, literary prizes,
or publishers' advances came his way.

No explanation is adequate for some eccentricities—for
example, the personas that he adopted, elaborated, and
clung to. Consider only two of them. The first involved a
career in the Royal Air Force toward the end of the First
World War. Passing himself off as a British subject (with
the appropriate accent), he enlisted in Toronto and returned to Oxford after a few months in an RAF officer's
uniform and insignia (unearned) and stories of being shot
down over France and patched up with a silver plate in his
skull. He had never left the ground, though afterward he
did learn to fly after a fashion, threatening his own life and
that of others. Much later he took on the role of the Virginia aristocrat, huntsman, and horseman, complete with
fancy riding pants, scarlet jacket, black boots, and top hat.
He was described by a friend as a "terrible" rider, and the
smashed vertebrae and shattered bones that he sustained
from many frightful falls were not imaginary.

Problems of the sort already suggested were enough to
keep battalions of scholars busy for years, but there remained the more important questions of interpretation:
how to read what Faulkner wrote, and how to correct mis-
interpretations of it. What was he trying to tell us about

the South, old and new? As one of his own characters put it, *"What do they do there. Why do they live there. Why do they live at all?"* Was he selling us another romance in the guise of degeneration, the decline and fall of the old regime? Was he a racist in sheep's clothing? A cryptofascist? Or was he really speaking, as in his Nobel Prize address, of the human condition and its tragedy, "the human heart in conflict with itself," whether in Yoknapatawpha County or anywhere else in the world? Of the award, he said in his address that it was "made to me not as a man, but to my work—a life's work in the agony and sweat of the human spirit." But that work was about the South, about people living in its unique culture. Was it a new reading of Southern history?

Challenged by such questions, scholars filled the learned journals with articles and the shelves with books. For twenty or so years after Faulkner's death more was written about him and his works than about any other American novelist, living or dead. The attention rivaled that traditionally accorded to British classics by American academic and literary critics. After such a deluge, could there be anything of importance left to be said about the subject?

Joel Williamson in his *William Faulkner and Southern History* offers persuasive evidence, I think, that there are indeed some deeper understandings possible, and that historians are capable of adding insights to literary criticism. Williamson's book is primarily biographical, yet he would admit that for full and detailed information we must still depend heavily on the work of Joseph Blotner—his two-volume, two-thousand-page biography and the one-volume edition less than half that length. Williamson writes of Blotner's "vast and excellent labor," adding that the biographer's relations with the Faulkners became "deeply personal"; Faulkner spoke of him as "my spiritual son."

The largest part of Williamson's book, entitled "Biography," is almost as much a study of the writings as the part officially devoted to the work. Its argument is that the story of the Faulkner clan and the novelist's Mississippi forebears, maternal as well as paternal, was "in effect, the real Yoknapatawpha County, the culture that made William Faulkner." That is not to say it made Faulkner's fiction: rather, it was the legend and reality on which Faulkner drew for the making of his fiction. Relating the one to the other, Williamson puts to rest the attempts to find in fact or fiction any reason for endowing Faulkner with an Old South background of planter aristocrats. Instead, both the forebears and the novels embody a South far more complex in varieties, classes, and styles of life. In addition to the Compsons and the Sartorises, there were the McCaslins and the Snopeses, as well as a memorable cast of black characters, all existing in a culture with mixtures of class and heredity, sexuality and miscegenation, violence and brutality, rascality and integrity.

Williamson begins with ancestry, 138 pages of it, dug out of county courthouse records, unpublished census data, and a dozen archives, "gold mines of information." To offer a sample of the riches: the first Mississippi Falkner (so spelled then) was William C. Falkner, the novelist's great-grandfather. As a penniless teenager he entered the state afoot about 1842, a fugitive from his hard-pressed Missouri family, who punished him for a bloody assault on his brother. He came in search of an uncle, John Wesley Thompson, who had moved to Mississippi in the 1830's after being acquitted of murder by a Georgia court. By the time of young Falkner's arrival on his doorstep in the town of Ripley, Thompson had made a good start in politics and law, and was able to help William begin his rapid rise. As a volunteer in the Mexican War, William suffered wounds in a hand and a foot, inflicted to avenge alleged insult to a woman. He returned home, entered the bar, and married a young woman who had inherited slaves. He bought land and appeared to be destined for a planter's life.

In 1849, however, his luck changed. In a fight he stabbed and killed a son of the wealthy Hindman family and was acquitted of murder. Two years later he shot and killed a friend of the Hindmans' and was again acquitted: two killings before he was twenty-five. A pistol duel between Falkner and the brother of the Hindman he had killed was arranged and narrowly averted. The feud continued, but by 1860 Falkner was a prosperous businessman, "not the richest man" in the county, "but he was well off." When war came, he was elected colonel of a regiment that acquitted itself well at Manassas. But embittered by failing to be reelected and failing to gain a brigadier's commission, the colonel "disappeared from view for almost two years," during which he seems to have been smuggling cotton across war borders in profitable if quite illegal and dangerous exchange for Yankee products.

With only a few slaves to emancipate and no plantation to lose, he emerged from the war and remained through

Reconstruction one of the richest men in his county. One of his numerous business enterprises was a railroad to connect by a short route the Gulf with the Great Lakes—a dream of empire in the robber-baron style. For his labor force, instead of Chinese coolies he leased state convicts at fifty dollars each per year, and he secured land and largess from the state legislature, with the help of the Congress and President Cleveland. In the meantime he wrote a melodramatic novel called *The White Rose of Memphis* that sold 160,000 copies after its publication in 1881 and might be reckoned among his business ventures.

Upon quarreling with his long-term partner Richard Thurmond, the colonel bought Thurmond's share of investment in the railroad and became its sole owner. But his feud continued for years, with exchanges of insults and court actions, and ended with Thurmond shooting Falkner down on a street in Ripley on November 5, 1889. He died the next day. Thurmond was acquitted of the murder "not so much by the brilliance of his lawyer," says Williamson, as because Falkner had over the years thoroughly "alienated himself from this community by his independence, his willfulness, and his egoism." It had been a veritable career of alienation in which "the people closest to him were the very people who cast him out," starting with his parents in Missouri. Anticipating his end, he had commissioned a larger-than-life statue of himself—made by an Italian sculptor in Carrara marble—which was placed atop a fourteen-foot pedestal, a monument that still marks his grave.

Struck by an "almost total neglect" of the Butlers, the

novelist's forebears on his mother's side, Williamson brings much new light to bear on the creation of the Yoknapatawpha legend. Like the Falkners, the Butlers were townsmen, hotel owners, and businessmen—not planters but well-off. For a sample of the Butler breed to match Colonel Falkner, we may turn to William Falkner's maternal grandfather, Charles E. Butler, who became head of the Butler clan as a youth. He was elected marshal of the town of Oxford in 1876, an office that turned into that of town manager, with the duties of collecting taxes and paying public debts. As a police officer he shot and killed Sam Thompson, the editor of a local newspaper, while attempting to arrest him in 1883. Thompson was known as a drunk and scofflaw, and he was drunk while resisting arrest. Butler was reelected town marshal before his trial, at which the jury found him not guilty.

For the next five years or so, life for the Butlers appeared on the surface to go smoothly. He and his artistic wife Lelia had two attractive teenage children who had been born quite early in the marriage. Charlie earned a good living and was well established in the community, probably owing in part to the high reputation of his father, the county's first sheriff, who had surveyed and laid out the town of Oxford. If he had the vices of drink or enjoyed riotous living, there was no record of it, nor any evidence of insolvency or neglect of official duties. He had been unanimously reelected by the aldermen in 1886, and had about completed the collection of town taxes for 1887 around Christmas, when he mysteriously and completely disappeared. Investigation by the aldermen in February,

1888, concluded that Charlie had absconded with "a shockingly large amount of town money," deserted his wife and children, and left his bondsmen responsible for missing funds. He never returned.

Williamson offers an explanation for Butler's disappearance; it introduces an important racial theme of his book, a theme that also enters significantly into his interpretation of Colonel Falkner, whose violent end came only two years after Butler absconded. As a historian of the South, Williamson has made race and racial mixing central to his interest. It seems likely that the prominence of these themes in Faulkner's work played a part in drawing the historian into a study of the author. He points out that "race was central, integral, and vital in the three great novels of the earlier phase of his work"—*The Sound and the Fury* (1929), *Light in August* (1932), and *Absalom, Absalom!* (1936). He adds that in the later novels, *Go Down, Moses* (1942), *Intruder in the Dust* (1948), and *Requiem for a Nun* (1951), race questions figure even more pointedly and powerfully.

Colonel Falkner had trouble getting along with his wife, and so did Charles Butler with his. The colonel's wife eventually moved to Memphis and stayed. Her husband was known to have a "shadow family," Emeline Falkner and three children, all born slaves and children of former owners, all very "white." Falkner bought them in 1858, and Emeline later bore him a daughter he named Fannie Forrest Falkner. To this daughter Falkner remained strongly attached. He sent Fannie to Rust College, a Mississippi school for blacks, where he visited her and brought her flowers, and where immediately after her graduation in 1888 she married the man who was later to become president of the college for many years. Before the college years, however, Emeline and Fannie had made an astonishing if temporary change of residence, and they were listed in the 1880 census as "Servant" and "House Maid," respectively, in the household of Richard Thurmond, the man who was to shoot and kill Falkner in December, 1889. Emeline and her first two daughters are buried a few yards from the towering statue of the colonel in the Ripley cemetery. So much for Great-Grandfather Falkner.

About Grandfather Butler, the evidence regarding marital, extramarital, and interracial history is much more circumstantial, but it is regarded by Williamson as "fairly strong." Tradition had it that Charlie not only went bankrupt but ran away with a "beautiful octoroon." We are given reason to discard the theory of bankruptcy, but we are clearly expected to take more seriously the "beautiful octoroon." She is described without further explanation as the "companion" of the wife of Jacob Thompson of Oxford, "model of the cotton frontier aristocrat," a wealthy planter and a personal friend of President Buchanan and a member of his cabinet. History, census data, family tradition, interviews, legend, rumor, and hearsay are pressed into service in support of the theory concerning the octoroon, which is usually hedged about with qualifying "if"s. But in a section entitled "Maybe," thus begging license for speculation, caution is all but abandoned. In a single paragraph there appear two "chances are," one "it might be," and one "he might," not to mention a "possibly,"

a "perhaps," and a "probably," all leading up to an elaboration of a theory the tenor of which is to make "it
seem likely that the couple had children"—slightly off-
color half brothers and half sisters of Muriel, mother of the
novelist, so that Faulkner's cousins included "the ensuing
generation."

It is enough to bring half the academic historians to their
feet with cries of indignation. As a member of the guild, I
understand their complaint. As a reader of Faulkner, however, I beg an exception to the rules, and a generous effort
to understand what our colleague is about. He writes in
one place that "this is not the world that William Faulkner
created; it is, rather, the world that created William Faulkner." Yet he also knows that before Billy Falkner became William Faulkner, and even after that, he lived with
family tradition and community gossip that filled in gaps
or left awkward subjects to the imagination, out of which
he created both his "real" and his fictional world. Even if
much of it was rumor, it was formative material for the
novelist.

Faulkner's parents moved to Oxford when he was five,
and memories of absconding Grandfather Butler were still
alive in that community: "his absence amounted almost to
a perpetual—and painful—presence in the household in
which William Faulkner grew up." That household, however, provided Billy with a devoted mother and a suppor-
tive father. Courthouse Square in Oxford was the stage for
much family drama—site of the old Butler Hotel and
nearby the spot where Grandfather Butler shot Sam
Thompson to death. Community feelings against a mis-

great grandfather in Oxford recalled to Billy the bitterness against a great-grandfather in Ripley, where he had seen people cross the street to avoid speaking to his parents. Whether the truly historical world or the writer's fictional world was the stranger and the more incredible was often a toss-up. From the tension between the two, and the pressure of being "always an outsider observing critically the social universe to which he was born" sprang "the power of the artist" and, according to Williamson, "both sustenance and pain."

Family legend and history did not end with great-grandfathers and grandfathers but continued with a repetition of early themes, including violence, down to events within the novelist's time. His own father, Murry Falkner, after winning a fight in his youth over a woman, was shot in the back the next day by his rival, who then turned him over and shot him in the mouth. He somehow survived. Many years later a small grandson asked him why he slipped a pistol into his pocket before taking the boy to see a circus. The reply was that he "might see that fellow."

Faulkner's huge cast of fictional characters was by no means limited to those resembling relatives or ancestors or their slaves, but those who do suggest such origins cover a wide variety of classes and types. His own Uncle John was said by a cousin to be as "crooked as a barrel of snakes," and by Williamson to be "more than a match for any ambitious redneck—any 'Snopes.'" The Snopes trilogy—*The Hamlet* (1940), *The Town* (1957), and *The Mansion* (1959)—could not have been set, of course, anywhere but in Yoknapatawpha County, but we are rightly warned against assuming that they, or any of Faulkner's novels, were written to depict or to characterize the South or its people. He just happened to know the South well enough to write about it, he explained to Cowley, but "man stinks the same stink no matter where in time"—or in place, he could have added. What was often taken as an apology for the South was really an indictment not only of the South but of America.

His own time, however, coincided with the crest of radical racist hysteria in the South and left its mark on the man and his work. He could slip into a rhetorical slur against blacks, but he was no bigot and hated bigotry. Nor could he be called a liberal. Yet in his major novels from 1932 to *Go Down, Moses* in 1942, he anticipated the revolt against racism by his scorn of stereotypes and the moral stature and individuality he accorded his black characters. In 1943 he called on Americans to "make good the shibboleths they glibly talk about freedom, liberty, human rights" and predicted that "change will come out of this war." His *Intruder in the Dust* (1948), addressing race relations, was his most popular novel but not among his best. Nor was *A Fable* (1954), which confronted war as a public issue. In his new persona as savant, pundit, and reformer, Faulkner proved even more inept than he was in air combat and horsemanship. After the *Brown* decision against school segregation in 1954 he increasingly exposed himself in the press with contradictory, confused, and ultimately reactionary positions on race that provided ridicule, embarrassed his friends, and plunged him into cycles of heavy drinking that landed him in the hospital vomiting blood.

A personal life so crowded with contradiction and paradox, and a body of writings so cryptic and enigmatic, make it all but impossible to venture a generalization about either the man or his work without risk of challenge by authorities. And venturing any theory about the relation of the man to his work runs equal risks. Undaunted, if uneasily aware of the hazards involved, Williamson has nevertheless undertaken these tasks, and I turn to Cleanth Brooks, a great authority on Faulkner, for the best justification I know of Williamson's linkage of Faulkner with Southern history. Any reader of the novels who expects enlightenment about history in the usual sense will be disappointed. Faulkner himself read little history, and deeply though his works were enmeshed in the past, they could not be called historical novels. According to Brooks, Faulkner viewed "the past as a living force in the present, a force that moulds our sense of the present," and also held that "time does not exist apart from the consciousness of some human being." Faulkner could say in an interview that "there is only the present moment, in which I include both the past and the future." Later, in referring to "my own theory that time is a fluid condition," he would add, "there is no such thing as *was*—only *is*."

More than once Faulkner would mention Henri Bergson in support of his theory about the fluidity of time and the presence of the past in the present. But then he would later throw in Gustave Flaubert, Honoré de Balzac, and Marcel Proust for good measure. In the opinion of Brooks, Faulkner never read Bergson very deeply but merely found in him "confirmation, from a respected philosopher, of something that he already knew," an assumption on which he had proceeded from the start, "that to isolate the past from the present was to falsify the very nature of time." The folk culture in which he grew up, and which he wrote about, had a powerful sense of the past, history not from books but, as Brooks puts it, "absorbed through a process of cultural osmosis." As Faulkner himself described his sources of Southern history, "I was just saturated with it, but never read about it."

This does not imply either disparagement or justification of the present or nostalgia for past glories, and it certainly carries no implication of "progress." There were those who used history to fabricate such myths, but William Faulkner was not one of them.

13

The Burden for
Robert Penn Warren

NO DEATH IN RECENT YEARS LEFT SO LARGE A PLACE TO BE
filled in American literary life as that created by the passing of Robert Penn Warren. Well before the end he had
come to be recognized as our most eminent living man of
letters. That is not to be explained by any one masterpiece
or mastery of any one literary form—though mastery and
masterpieces were in evidence—but rather by brilliance,
versatility, boldness, and originality in an extraordinary variety of forms. In addition to poetry and novels these included the short story, the essay, literary and social criticism, biography, and works of historical reflection. Writing
went forward in all these forms while he was actively engaged in teaching, editing journals, and producing famous
guides and texts for the study of literature. In all, the total,
apart from textbooks and literary guidebooks, came to
forty volumes, including sixteen in poetry and eleven in
fiction.

While Warren practiced all these arts more or less simultaneously, the balance of productivity shifted from one literary form to another during a writing career of more than

sixty years. At first he was thought of primarily as a splendid novelist who also wrote some good poetry. In those years appeared his most powerful and exciting novels, including *Night Rider* (1939), *At Heaven's Gate* (1943), *All the King's Men* (1946), and *World Enough and Time* (1950). These plus six others to come won him national and international fame and just about all the awards and prizes by which novelists are honored.

A busy interlude, beginning in the 1950's and continuing into the 1960's, followed, during which, though fiction and verse continued to flow, Warren was diverted to some extent by the Civil War centennial and the civil rights movement into works of nonfiction and meditative essays. These included *Segregation: The Inner Conflict of the South* (1956) and *The Legacy of the Civil War: Meditations on the Centennial* (1961), two profound essays.

It was after this period and during the last two and a half decades of his life that Warren experienced the remarkable regeneration of creativity, the late flowering in poetic form that assured his solitary eminence. The new period would seem associated with his marriage to the writer Eleanor Clark and the birth of their daughter, Rosanna, and their son, Gabriel. Ten of his sixteen volumes of poetry and most of his greatest poems came forth in these years. They include *Incarnations: Poems, 1966–1968* (1968), *Audubon: A Vision* (1969), the transforming revision of *Brother to Dragons* (1979), and *Chief Joseph of the Nez Perce* (1983), as well as six superb collections of the shorter poems between 1974 and 1985. In the transition from being foremost a novelist to preeminence as a poet, Warren has been compared to Thomas Hardy, a writer he admired, and in the late full flowering of poetic genius not only to Hardy but to Wallace Stevens, William Carlos Williams, and William Butler Yeats. This, to be sure, is high praise. Along with it has come some critical disparagement for outmoded diction and mannered style. Less of this dissent was heard, however, as the outpouring of verse reached new heights instead of diminishing and as accolade followed accolade—the Bollingen Prize in Poetry, Pulitzer prizes in both poetry and fiction, the Presidential Medal of Freedom, and in 1986 designation as the first Poet Laureate of his country.

Born and reared in rural southwest Kentucky, Warren went to college at Vanderbilt, where he became a precocious member of the Fugitive poets and later the Agrarians. He left the South for graduate work at Berkeley, Yale, and Oxford but returned in 1930 and tried unsuccessfully to establish himself in academic life at three institutions, the last being Louisiana State University. Failing to find satisfactory roots and feeling unwanted Warren left the South in 1942, the outset of his most productive years, never to return save for visits. He spent most of his exile years at Yale, or living nearby, but he remained almost as much a self-conscious exile from the South as James Joyce was from Ireland—and also nearly as preoccupied in his writings with his native region for the rest of his life as Joyce was with Ireland.

The South furnished the setting for virtually all of Warren's fiction and much of his poetry as well as the subject of his nonfictional prose. It never occurred to him, he said, that he "could write about anything except life in the South." He disclaimed "any romantic notions about it." It was simply that he was "naturally steeped in it" and "knew that world" as he knew no other and, like Allen Tate's, it was a "knowledge carried to the heart." His was not a South as confined as Faulkner's "postage stamp" of a Mississippi county, but it rarely ranged beyond the western parts of Kentucky and Tennessee for source and setting of either verse or fiction. Events of 1811 became the subject of *Brother of Dragons,* and events of the 1820s inspired *World Enough and Time.* These and most later events that became subjects of his books took place, he said, "around my home section" and inspired a wealth of folklore and legend that enriched his childhood imagination.

Warren's work is rightly identified as part of the Southern Literary Renaissance, and an outstanding part it is. It undoubtedly shares traits of that school, including the violence in which his subjects were often involved. But he was distinctive in the outlook and philosophy that inspired him. In these respects he was somewhat closer to Joseph Conrad than to William Faulkner. Warren was a master of the ironic and the oxymoronic. He is constantly reminding us of the contrast between the intent and the result of human motives and plans, between expectation and the outcome. Evil often results from good and vice versa. Misanthropy becomes philanthropy and philanthropy self-love. Heroes turn out to be villainous and the other way around. Worthy and even noble causes resort to terrorism and bloody deeds.

These paradoxical themes run through many of Warren's works from the earliest of them on down through the years. His first book, *John Brown* (1929), published when he was only twenty-three, announces the theme. Emerson, the paragon of Transcendentalism, and some of his disciples conspire with a murderous fanatic whose plot is a bloody disaster responsible for the death of followers and of himself, and whose deed heralds the approach of death for hundreds of thousands. In *Night Rider,* Warren's first novel, Perse Munn gains the reader's immediate admiration as a man of complete integrity, enlightened, gracious, and generous, the perfect Southern gentleman to whom his community naturally turns for leadership in time of crisis. In the struggles for justice against forces of oppression that follow, however, Munn to his own bewilderment repudiates and desecrates all he has stood for by acts of atrocity, betrayal, murder, and brutality in pursuit of justice and self-knowledge—neither of which he gains. Disintegration and death end the quest.

Paradoxes of good and evil take varied forms. In *All the King's Men,* as in some of the other novels, is a superimposed short story, this one of ante bellum times, that prefigures more complex ironies in a novel about twentieth-century events. Cass Mastern, great-uncle of the narrator of the novel, Jack Burden, and the subject of his doctoral dissertation in history, is an innocent and virtuous young man who has an affair with the wife of his best friend and benefactor. The betrayal results in the destruction of three lives. Cass then expiates his guilt by martyrdom in fighting for the Confederate cause, in which he does not believe. Jack Burden comes eventually to understand the meaning of Cass Mastern's tragedy through the recovery of his own past and acknowledgment of his own share of guilt in the suicide of his father, the assassination of Willie Stark, and the killing of his friend Adam Stanton. He also realizes that the idealist in Jack Burden that bound him to Willie Stark in order to "do good" has plunged him into the sum of evils, while Stark's belated impulse to do good "with clean hands" assures his quietus.

In Warren's poetry the most memorable example of an idealist confronting evil is the book-length dramatic dialogue *Brother to Dragons*. Here Thomas Jefferson, framer of his nation's ideals and hopes at its birth, meditates with "R.P.W." and his own sister Lucy Jefferson Lewis upon the horrible crime of her sons, the president's nephews, Lilburne and Isham, at their home in Kentucky in 1811. In the meat-house, where he assembled all the slaves, Lilburne had murdered and butchered into pieces on the meat block a sixteen-year-old slave named George, who had broken a pitcher that had belonged to Lucy. As in *All the King's Men*, the dominant theme is the necessity of accepting the past, no matter how terrible. "For without the fact of the past we cannot dream the future," concludes Jefferson.

None of these chilling reflections, here or in any of Warren's work, may be construed as cynicism about human relations. Jefferson remains a great man at the conclusion of *Brother to Dragons*. Nor does the total impact of Warren's lifework suggest a nihilistic view of history, nor any variety of historical inevitability or determinism. Nor does it imply that the course of history lies beyond human influence or that mankind ever escapes responsibility for guilt by blaming it all on history. And neither was Warren one to evade moral issues or dismiss as do-gooders those who attempt to improve man's lot.

The poet himself never retreated into pursuit of his art to shun grave social struggles of his time. His sunset hawk soars to incredible heights but it always returns to earth. In fact quite earthly concerns, especially over racial injustice in the South and in America at large, found place in novels such as *Band of Angels* (1955), *Wilderness* (1961), and *Flood* (1964), and in some poems of those years. More to the point are two works of nonfiction addressed entirely to the issue and written in response to the civil rights movement: *Segregation: The Inner Conflict of the South* (1956) and *Who Speaks for the Negro?* (1965). *Segregation* uses narrative, interview, and reflection to dramatize the moral struggles of the author and his native region and the excitement of history in the making. At the start Warren repudiates views expressed in an essay of 1930 for *I'll Take My Stand* and embraces the new movement for racial justice. In the book of 1965 the stage is turned over to the victims of injustice and their spokesmen or to interviews and dialogue with them—all save the conclusion, which is a self-interview. Declaring that "we have to deal with the problem our historical moment proposes, the burden of our time," Warren refused to retreat from moral responsibility in the name of Southern tradition and continuity. Instead he called on the South to furnish leadership in repudiating the old order and advancing the new and believed it would do so.

Writers of the Southern Renaissance have long been noted for consciousness of the past in the present, but with Warren history was a special passion. He refused to be called an historical novelist or writer, even though a number of his best novels and major poems are focused on historical events, conflicts, or figures. But history was for him much more than a source of subject matter: it was the foundation of his world view and his values on which all his work was built. He read deeply, not only in classical historians but in modern works. He knew, as he wrote in "Wind and Gibbon," that "history is not truth. Truth is in the telling." In the essay "The Use of the Past," he asked if anyone could "read a page of Tacitus or Gibbon without being struck anew by the irony of good and evil interfused in our nature." For him, "The sense of the past and the sense of the present are somehow intertwined constantly." They would seem to be intertwined in all he wrote.

In *The Legacy of the Civil War* Warren said that this conflict was, "for the American imagination, the great single event of our history." Whatever we make of it, "the War grows in our consciousness. The event stands there larger than life, massively symbolic in its inexhaustible and sybilline significance." It was, he wrote, "our Homeric period," filled with legendary figures and scenes as well as tormenting confusions and brutal ambivalence. We continue to grope for its meaning with the yearning that some of its tragic dignity and grandeur may rub off on us. Such yearning, in the present as in a remote past, in this instance as in prehistory, is best served by the poet rather than the historian. It is our great fortune that we had among us for a time a poet who understood that—and so much else about his role and about his art.

Index